Barbara-jo McIntosh

TIN FISH
GOURMET

Great Seafood from Cupboard to Table

RAINCOAST BOOKS

Vancouver

First published in 1998 by

Raincoast Books
8680 Cambie Street
Vancouver, B. C.
v6p 6m9
(604) 323-7100

2 3 4 5 6 7 8 9 10

CANADIAN CATALOGUING IN PUBLICATION DATA

McIntosh, Barbara-jo.
  Tin Fish Gourmet

  Includes index.
  ISBN 1-55192-158-8

  1. Cookery (Fish) I. Title.

TX747.M34 1998   641.6'92   c97-910979-5

Printed in Canada

Raincoast Books gratefully acknowledges the support of the Government of Canada through the Book Publishing Industry Development Program, the Canada Council, the Department of Canadian Heritage and the British Columbia Arts Council.

CONTENTS

ACKNOWLEDGEMENTS

SPECIAL THANKS to Carol Watterson, for pushing the project; Ruth Wilson, for perceptive proofing; Brian Scrivener, for sharp vision and wit; Rachelle Kanefsky, for fabulous fish factoids; Jacqueline Ehlert, for nutritional input; Frank and David, for culinary assistance; Michelle, Dan, Veryl and John, for their constant support; and my mother, for almost everything.

I would also like to thank the following people for the use of their private collections of tin fish labels: Christina Burridge, B.C. Salmon Marketing Council, Vancouver; Roger Porter, Vancouver, B.C.; and Bernard Spring, Vancouver, B.C.

INTRODUCTION

FISH HAS BEEN a part of my life since I was five years old. At the time, my divorced mother began to date a man named Roy who was a commercial fisherman in the summer and a hairdresser in the winter. We began to eat a lot of fish, and we all had great hair. I remember learning how to shuck oysters at the age of six. I remember crying at the sight of all those baby fishes inside the mommy fishes' tummies when we cleaned them, feeling responsible for their deaths because we had cut the mother fishes open. Eventually, I got over it and ate a lot more fish.

This included tin fish, of course. Such classic tin fish dishes as tuna casserole, salmon loaf and shrimp curry became my childhood versions of comfort food. The tins themselves, stacked in the cupboard to form colourful towers, were an essential part of our kitchen pantry. And, even then, I was well aware of the ease and convenience they provided.

I was also well aware of the process that went into creating tin fish. When my brother turned 14, he started to go fishing with Roy in the summer. Tales of the northern regions of British Columbia – the eagles, the ocean and, of course, very large fish – swam through our dinner-table conversation in great abundance.

Growing up, I was lucky to experience some magical places of my own. Vancouver's Campbell Avenue Fisherman's Wharf was an incredible place. As a young girl, I was overwhelmed by the exotic smells, the sturdy boats, the large totes of fish and the interesting array of dockside characters. Tearfully, I would watch as my big brother set sail for the summer. I longed to be out on the water, casting my own net.

As the years moved on, my brother left his studies at college to become a full-time fisherman, and I took a job in the fishing industry. Naturally, I fell in love with a man who shared my passion for seafood, so there was always more fish to eat and enjoy. I happily began to experiment with ways of preparing fish. But, no matter how sophisticated my recipes became, I never forgot how to use a can opener.

I even spent some time living in a suite over a fish canning plant. I found watching the tins of fish moving along the line – with the help of so many like-minded people – to be far more interesting than television. I guess, once you're a fish person, it never really leaves you.

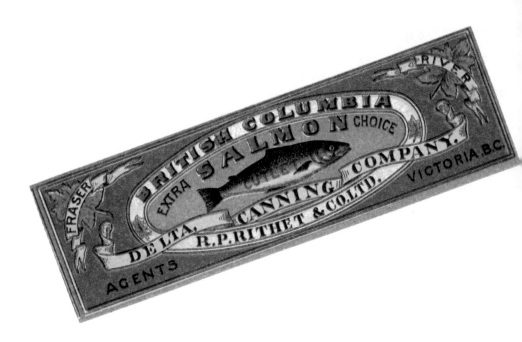

Years later, I tore myself away from the fish business to explore various aspects of the restaurant and hospitality industry. After many years of learning from the masters, I went out on my own. But, no matter what I did, thoughts of fish were never very far away. It didn't matter whether I was running my own catering company, organizing unique and splendiferous events or starting my own restaurant.

Appropriately enough, my restaurant's name was Barbara-jo's. Although fish was not the predominant theme, it was somehow also appropriate that the most popular dish turned out to be crabcakes. Other wonderful dishes included baked salmon with a roasted vegetable salsa, bourbon prawns, oyster and artichoke stew, seared scallops with a lime and ginger sauce and steamed clams and mussels with a tomato and wine cilantro broth.

But, even as a restaurant owner, I always felt that you shouldn't have to journey far for the privilege of enjoying fish. It's much too wonderful an experience to be limited to those times when your wallet's fat or you simply feel like stepping out to eat. What if you've decided to spend an extra day at the cottage?

What if you're simply too tired after a hard day at the office to do much more than open a cupboard? And so *Tin Fish Gourmet* was born.

These economical recipes – tin fish combined with various ingredients that are readily available in any well-stocked cupboard – are updated versions of the recipes I loved as a child. In these lean and mean times, they're designed for those moments when you want to raid the cupboard for a quick, hearty and healthy – and wonderful – meal.

I hope you find strength, comfort and enjoyment in this book. It's written for everyone who enjoys good quality tin fish prepared in a simple, tasty and creative fashion. And it is dedicated with affection to all those in my fishy past.

MAYON
BRAND

IN TOMATO SAUCE

PACKED
SARDINE
STYLE

ANCHOVIES
IN TOMATO SAUCE
PACKED FROM THE CHOICEST
FISH IN CALIFORNIA COAST

ANCHOVIES

THIS MISUNDERSTOOD morsel deserves so much more credit than it gets. Although many gourmets consider the anchovy to be an essential ingredient in a true Caesar salad, some people are a little intimidated by this salty little fish. (Hence cries of "Hold the anchovies!" are often heard when a large group decides to order pizza.) But in countries all over the world the anchovy is highly respected.

In North America small herringlike fish such as sprats, pilchards and alewives are often used in place of true anchovies. The real anchovy, however, is only about 7 cm (3 in) long and is found in abundance in the Mediterranean as well as off the warm shores of California and Peru. Because the anchovy's tender white flesh deteriorates quickly when exposed to air, many people have never actually tasted the fish served fresh. The anchovy must be heavily salted in order to be preserved, and it is often packed in oil. This can create a problem for those on a sodium-restricted diet, those with gout or high blood pressure or those watching their cholesterol.

But they need not avoid anchovies altogether. A good way to reduce their saltiness and oiliness is by soaking them in white wine or milk prior to using them in a recipe. Anchovies also contain niacin and omega-3 monounsaturated fats, as well as healthy quantities of iron and vitamin B_{12}. Used sparingly, anchovies can yield magnificent results.

ANCHOVY BUTTER

I THINK the nicest thing to have in the freezer is a prepared butter that will accent numerous dishes. This butter is wonderful tossed on pasta or served with grilled steak, chicken or a strong-flavoured fish like salmon or tuna. You just cut 1/3 inch/8 mm of roll per serving and, voilà! Dinner is served!

1	1.75-oz/50 g tin anchovy fillets	1
1 lb	butter, softened	500 g
2	shallots, finely chopped	2
1/2 cup	flat leaf parsley, chopped	125 mL
1/2 cup	pimento, diced	125 mL

Place all ingredients in the bowl of a food processor with steel blade. Pulse until all ingredients are
uniformly distributed throughout the butter.

Take 16 inches/40 cm of waxed paper and lay
lengthwise on a clean work surface. Place all the
anchovy butter 1/3 of the way up the wax paper. Fold
the end nearest you up over the butter and roll to
form a uniform 2-inch/5 cm cylinder. Tightly wrap
the ends. Wrap again with plastic wrap and place in
freezer.

Anchovy paste spread

on bread and butter at

teatime was a favourite

in Victorian England.

ANCHOVY DRESSING FOR ROMAINE GREENS

YOU may want to call this Caesar salad dressing, but this version is much more adaptable. I often add all sorts of interesting ingredients to this dressing, such as roasted eggplant, roasted red pepper or carmelized onions.

1	1.75-oz/50 g tin anchovies	1
1 tbsp	capers	15 mL
1	lemon, zested and juiced	1
2 cups	mayonnaise	500 mL
1/4 cup	white wine vinegar	50 mL
2 tbsp	balsamic vinegar	25 mL
2 cloves	garlic, peeled and sliced	2
1/4 cup	olive oil	50 mL
	Salt	
	Fresh ground pepper	
2 heads	romaine lettuce, chopped, washed and spun dry	2
1/4 cup	grated Parmesan cheese	50 mL

In the bowl of a food processor with a steel blade, place the anchovies with oil, capers, lemon zest and juice, mayonnaise and the vinegars.

In a small frying pan, lightly cook the sliced garlic and olive oil over medium-high heat until the garlic smells sweet but is not browned (it will be bitter).

Turn on the food processor and purée the mayonnaise mixture. With machine running, add the hot garlic and oil. Process until smooth. Stop machine and taste. Add salt and pepper, if desired.

Toss mayonnaise mixture with washed salad greens and sprinkle with Parmesan cheese to garnish.

Recipe can be cut in half. However, dressing will keep in the fridge for well over a week.

ROSEMARY SCALLOPED POTATOES WITH ANCHOVIES AND GARLIC

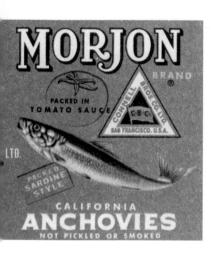

2 cloves	garlic, peeled	2
3	anchovy fillets	3
1/2 tsp	salt	2 mL
2/3 cup	whipping cream	150 mL
10 drops	Tabasco sauce	10
1/2 tsp	dried rosemary, crumbled	2 mL
3 to 4	potatoes, scrubbed	3 to 4
	Fresh ground black pepper	

Preheat the oven to 375°F/190°C. Place rack in the lower third of oven.

Lightly butter a small casserole dish.

Coarsely chop the garlic with the anchovies and salt until you have a pasty mixture. Set aside.

In a small bowl mix the whipping cream, Tabasco and crumbled rosemary. Stir to combine evenly.

Slice the potatoes quite thin. Line the bottom of the casserole with 2 to 3 layers of potatoes. Place 1 tbsp/15 mL of anchovy mixture over the potatoes, then alternate one layer of potatoes with mixture until you have none left.

Top all layers with the cream mixture and fresh ground pepper to taste.

Bake covered for 45 minutes, uncover and bake for 10 more minutes. If potatoes are tender, your dish is done.

Allow to rest for about 5 minutes before serving.

Serves 2

ANCHOVY AND CHICK PEA PIZZA

NOTHING COULD be easier than this recipe. Rosemary best complements the flavourful anchovy because of its strong taste.

This is not a traditional pizza, and it is quite crumbly. But it's a tasty appetizer with your favourite brew!

2	anchovy fillets	2
1	14-oz/398 mL can chick peas, drained	1
1/2 tsp	dried or 2 tsp/10 mL fresh rosemary, crumbled	2 mL
1 tbsp	olive oil	15 mL

Preheat oven to 375°F/190°C.

In a food processor, mix the chick peas and anchovies to a paste. Spread mixture onto a pizza pan. Sprinkle with the chopped rosemary and drizzle the olive oil over the mixture. Bake for 20 minutes.

Serves 1 to 4

Canning was invented in France in 1809 by Nicholas Apert, who won first prize in a food preservation contest launched by the French government in 1795. With his prize money, Apert opened the first commercial cannery in the world.

REDSKIN
SALMON EGGS

NET WT. 3 OZ.

PACKED BY
WIEGARDT BROS.
OCEAN PARK, WASH. U.S.A.

CAVIAR

Mention the word *caviar* and visions of champagne, black ties and the Waldorf Astoria come to mind. Caviar seems synonymous with high society, but believe it or not, the real caviar craze only came to the Western world in 1920 when two Russo-Armenian brothers, Melkom and Mougcheg Petrossian, presented the product at the Gastronomic Exhibition at the Grand Palais in Paris. It was received, needless to say, with great enthusiasm.

Real caviar is made from the roe of various species of sturgeon. Interestingly enough, in mid-19th century North America a sturgeon wasn't worth more than about 10 cents. Nowadays the roe of the sturgeon is one of the most expensive food products in the world. Here in North America we can easily get our hands on imitation caviar, which is produced from the eggs of other fish, such as salmon, whitefish, lumpfish and cod. While not the "real thing," the good news is that these caviars are more affordable and can be just as interesting in texture and taste as sturgeon caviar. And, in even better news, caviar is a tasty indulgence that isn't bad for you! Five hundred grams (a little over 1 lb) of caviar contains only 68 g of fat and only 1,188 calories (74 calories per oz). And while it may seem a bit salty, 30 g (1 oz) of caviar contains only about a third of the recommended daily allowance of sodium.

Whitefish, or golden, caviar from Canada's Great Lakes makes up a large part of the processed roe served in North American restaurants and homes. Personally, I like to use salmon or lumpfish caviars in my recipes, but any one of the tasty fish roes available at your neighbourhood supermarket will make a memorable and mouthwatering dish.

PASTA WITH ASPARAGUS, MUSHROOMS AND CAVIAR

MOST PEOPLE think of caviar as something to be enjoyed on its own. This recipe, however, is a perfect example of "fusion cooking," showing how well caviar can blend with a variety of other ingredients from around the globe. The asparagus is not just for show — it is a good low-calorie source of folic acid as well as the potent antioxidant vitamins A and C, and it's high in fibre.

4 tsp	caviar: salmon or lumpfish, or some of each if you have both	20 mL
4 oz	bow tie pasta	125 g
3 tbsp	olive oil	45 mL
1	red onion, peeled and sliced	1
1	clove garlic, chopped	1
6	shiitake mushrooms, stems removed and caps sliced	6
6	spears asparagus, woody parts trimmed and tender parts cut into 1 1/2-inch/3.5 cm pieces	6
2 oz	sun-dried tomatoes, sliced	56 g
	Juice of 1 lemon	
2 tbsp	sour cream (or yogourt)	25 mL
	Salt	
	Fresh ground black pepper	
	Chives (optional)	

Preheat oven to 400°F/200°C. Cook the pasta according to the package instructions, drain and set aside.

In medium-size saucepan over medium-high heat, add olive oil then the onion. Sauté for a couple of minutes then roast in oven for 4 minutes. Add the garlic and mushrooms. Stir well and return to the oven for about 4 more minutes. Stir once more.

Add the asparagus spears and the sun-dried tomatoes. Roast for another 4 minutes or until the asparagus is just tender. Remove from the oven and toss with the cooked, drained pasta and lemon juice. Serve into 2 bowls, top with sour cream and the caviar. Salt and pepper to taste and garnish with chopped chives if available.

Serves 2

Because it is produced via the reproductive process, caviar has been considered an aphrodisiac for centuries. In fact, all fish products have been, in one way or another, somehow connected with that wily goddess of love and beauty, Aphrodite. According to legend, anything that comes from the sea, Aphrodite's birthplace, should bear her power.

WARM ENDIVE, POTATO AND AVOCADO SALAD WITH CAVIAR DRESSING

THIS IS quite possibly the most sophisticated salad recipe ever created, an honour largely due to the addition of caviar in the dressing. If you don't live in a penthouse overlooking Manhattan, this dish will make you feel like you do!

1 to 2 tbsp	caviar	15 to 25 mL
4 or 5	Belgian endives, bottoms trimmed to separate the leaves easily	4 or 5
2	ripe Roma tomatoes, sliced 1/4-inch/0.5 cm thick	2
1	avocado, diced	1
1	russet potato, scrubbed	1
1/3 cup	olive oil	75 mL
3	shallots or 1/2 white onion, peeled and finely chopped	3
	Dash salt	
	Fresh ground black pepper	
2 tbsp	white wine vinegar	25 mL

Place the Belgian endives in a salad bowl. Add tomato slices and avocado. Toss to combine and set aside.

Pierce potato 3 or 4 times and microwave 3 to 4 minutes until just cooked through.

Heat the olive oil in a small fry pan over medium heat, add the chopped shallots and sauté for 2 minutes. Slice the cooked potato into ¹/4-inch/ 0.5 cm slices and add to the shallots. Add salt and fresh ground pepper to taste. Cook for another 2 minutes. Remove from the heat and add the vinegar and the caviar. Shake the pan to mix together. Pour over the prepared salad ingredients. Toss to coat well.

Serves 2

While early Persians believed that *chav-jar*, "cake of strength," cured hangovers, and Russians claimed that it cured impotence and constipation, today we know that caviar contains 47 vitamins and minerals, as well as acetylcholine, a substance that has been linked to increased alcohol tolerance.

SCRAMBLED EGGS WITH SALMON CAVIAR

THE ADDITION OF salmon caviar in this recipe dresses up a breakfast standard. If you are like me, you'll enjoy this dish with a glass of champagne.

2 oz	salmon caviar	56 g
6	large eggs	6
2 tbsp	water	25 mL
1 tbsp	butter	15 mL
1 tbsp	olive oil	15 mL
1 tbsp	chopped chives	15 mL
	Salt	
	Fresh ground pepper	
2 tbsp	sour cream	25 mL

In a bowl whisk together eggs and water.

In a medium-size fry pan over medium heat, melt the butter and olive oil until bubbly. Add the egg mixture and let set for a moment. With a spatula, gently distribute the egg mixture about the pan. After the first stir, add the chives. After the second stir, add $3/4$ of the caviar. By this time the eggs should be set but not dry. Transfer to warm serving plates, season with salt and pepper and dollop with sour cream and the remaining caviar.

Serves 2

It takes 20 years for the female beluga to yield eggs, which partly explains the rarity and high cost of beluga caviar. Due to an alarming drop in sturgeon populations, Russian scientists have perfected a type of caesarean operation that enables them to remove the roe and then throw the fish back into the water alive to begin the reproduction process again.

WILD RICE PANCAKES WITH SOUR CREAM AND CAVIAR

THE rice gives this recipe a satisfying crunch, quickly followed by the smoothness of caviar rolling over your tongue.

2 oz	caviar	56 g
1/2 cup	flour	125 mL
1 tsp	baking powder	5 mL
	Sprinkle of salt	
3/4 cup	buttermilk	175 mL
1	egg	1
3 tbsp	vegetable oil, divided	45 mL
3/4 cup	cooked wild rice	175 mL
2 tsp	fresh thyme, chopped	10 mL
1/2 tsp	lemon zest	2 mL
3/4 cup	sour cream	175 mL

Combine the flour, baking powder and salt in a mixing bowl. In another bowl, whisk together the buttermilk, egg and 2 tbsp/25 mL oil. Add to the dry ingredients and stir until combined. Fold in wild rice, fresh thyme and lemon zest.

Heat 1 tbsp/15 mL oil in fry pan until bubbly. Using a soup spoon, drop mixture into pan to form small pancakes. Cook until bubbles form over the surface. Turn over and cook until brown.

Remove to a warm plate and place in a 200°F/ 100°C oven until ready to serve. Place a dollop of sour cream on each pancake and top with the caviar.

Makes 18 to 24 pancakes

"There is more simplicity in the man who eats caviar on impulse than in the man who eats Grape-Nuts® on principle."

— G. K. CHESTERTON

CLAMS

I FIRST EXPERIENCED the convenience of cooking with tinned clams while preparing vast quantities of chowder in the high school cafeteria as part of my home economics course. I've always loved the challenge of digging for fresh clams on the beach. And one of the most romantic meals I ever had involved teaming a loaf of French bread and a bottle of white wine with steamed clams and garlic butter.

In North America there are three primary types of East Coast clams fished for human consumption: soft-shell clams, known as steamers, manninoses or squirts; hard-shell clams, identified as littlenecks, cherrystones, topneck clams, chowder clams and ocean quahogs; and surf clams, used mostly in packaged products like chowders, clam sauces and breaded clam strips. Native to the West Coast are pismo and butter clams, and both littlenecks and manila clams are cultivated in Washington State's Puget Sound area. The geoduck, found mostly in Washington and British Columbia, is the largest clam of the north Pacific. It can weigh up to 5 kg (11 lb) and live up to 150 years. This giant clam is harvested by divers and then canned, smoked, cooked in stews, eaten raw or fried up in steaks.

That said, making anything with tinned clams is much easier than using the fresh variety. The best news? When you buy good quality tinned clams, you can't beat the flavour.

CREAMY GARLIC
AND CLAM CHOWDER

WHEN I WAS in high school, my home economics course required me to cook clam chowder for the esteemed patrons of the cafeteria. My instructor, Miss Takach, was justly proud of her chowder recipe and I feel much the same about this adapted version with its accent on garlic. Long condemned as a social gaffe, garlic is undergoing a resurgence in popularity as researchers have found it plays a role in preventing cancer and lowering blood pressure and cholesterol.

1	5-oz/142 g tin baby clams, drained, reserving the liquid	1
6	garlic cloves, peeled	6
1	medium white onion, peeled and cut into quarters	1
1 tbsp	celery leaves, coarsely chopped	15 mL
1 tbsp	olive oil	15 mL
1 tbsp	dry sherry	15 mL
1	medium carrot, diced	1
1	stalk celery, diced	1
1	large russet potato, peeled and cut into ¹/₂-inch/1 cm cubes	1
1 tbsp	butter	15 mL
1 tbsp	flour	15 mL
1¹/₂ cups	milk	375 mL

The word *chowder*

probably derives from

the French *chaudière*,

a large pot into which

fishermen threw some

of the day's catch in

order to make fish stew.

Salt	
Fresh ground black pepper	
Green onions, sliced	

Preheat oven to 350°F/180°C.

In a 10-inch/25 cm casserole dish with lid, place the garlic, onion, celery leaves, oil and sherry. Toss together, cover and bake for 15 to 20 minutes. Remove from the oven and place over medium heat on top of the stove. Add the carrot, celery, potato and reserved clam juice. Bring to a boil, reduce heat and simmer 10 to 15 minutes until the potato is tender.

Meanwhile, in a small saucepan, melt the butter and add the flour. Combine well and cook for 1 minute, being careful not to brown. Slowly add the milk, stirring constantly to prevent lumps. Bring to a boil and cook for about 2 minutes until it starts to thicken.

Add the clams to the vegetable mixture, then add the milk sauce and stir to combine. Salt and pepper to taste and garnish with the sliced onions.

Serves 2 to 3

ARTICHOKE AND CLAM DIP

MY Definition of perfection? A quick and simple recipe that tastes as if you fussed over it. This dish is ideal for preparing at the last minute when unexpected guests drop by. Place dip in serving bowl. Serve with sesame crackers.

1	14-oz/398 mL tin artichokes in water, drained	1
1	5-oz/142 g tin baby clams, drained	1
1 cup	mayonnaise	250 mL
¼ tsp	cayenne pepper	1 mL
½ cup	grated Parmesan cheese	125 mL

Preheat oven to 375°F/190°C.

Place all ingredients in food processor fitted with steel blade. Blend until almost smooth. Place in an ovenproof dish and bake for 10 to 15 minutes until brown and bubbly.

Serves a small crowd

The first commercial cans were laboriously fashioned by hand. Cut from tinplate with hand shears, shaped on a wooden cylinder and soldered, the average production was 60 cans per man per day. Tops and bottoms were measured with a compass and also cut by hand and soldered. (Today hundreds of cans are produced every minute.)

CLAM AND FONTINA PIZZA

THe aroma of this dish as it bakes in the oven is a wonderful preamble to how it actually tastes. A favourite recipe for pizza dough adds to the fun. If you are short on time, try ready-made dough. Either way, this is a unique homemade treat.

Wooden pizza peels are available in most kitchen stores.

1	5-oz/142 g tin baby clams, drained	1
	Pizza dough for 1 pizza	
1/2 cup	tomato sauce	125 mL
1/4 cup	pesto sauce	30 mL
1 cup	grated fontina cheese	250 mL
1/4 cup	pine nuts, toasted	50 mL

Preheat oven to 500°F/290°C.

Place pizza stone in the oven on the middle rack and preheat for ¹/₂ hour. Flour your pizza peel and spread your dough on the peel. If using a baking sheet, spread it with cornmeal and place the dough on the baking sheet.

Spread the tomato sauce on the dough, then spoon the pesto sauce on top. Sprinkle the clams, pine nuts and, last, the fontina cheese over all.

Slide the pizza from the peel onto the hot stone and bake for 8 to 10 minutes or until the edges of the crust are nicely browned and the cheese evenly melted.

Serves 2 to 3

While all clams are born and mature as males, some change into females part way through life, giving a whole new meaning to mid-life crisis!

CLAMS AND STRAW MUSHROOMS OVER LINGUINI

REMEMBER THE DAYS when the only thing many families could imagine serving over pasta was meatballs the size of overgrown marbles? Thankfully, things have changed. This fusion dish, an Asian twist on an Italian staple, proves that mixing things up can add a little spice to life.

As popular as fresh pasta is these days, I prefer using dry linguini in this recipe.

1	5-oz/142 g tin baby clams, drained, reserving the liquid	1
2 tbsp	olive oil	25 mL
1/4 cup	onions, finely chopped	50 mL
5	cloves of garlic, chopped	5
3 tbsp	flat leaf parsley chopped, divided	45 mL
1/2 cup	white wine	125 mL
1	14-oz/298 mL tin straw mushrooms, drained and cut in half	1
1/2 lb	dry linguini	250 g

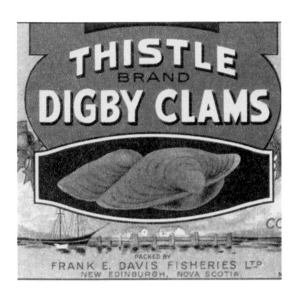

Cook the pasta according to the package instructions, drain and set aside.

In a medium to large fry pan, heat the olive oil over medium heat. Add the onions and garlic. Sauté for 2 to 3 minutes, being careful not to brown. Add 2 tbsp/25 mL of the parsley and the white wine and reduce for 1 minute. Add straw mushrooms and baby clams. Slowly add reserved clam liquid remaining until slightly reduced and heated through.

Toss over cooked linguini and serve. Garnish with remaining parsley.

Serves 2

ROASTED TOMATO AND CLAM CHOWDER

WHO DOESN'T LIKE a bowl of clam chowder on a crisp winter day? This version of a traditional recipe adds roasted tomatoes and pepper with balsamic vinegar, giving it a more robust touch. You can chop the ingredients as fine as you like. Personally, I prefer them a little on the chunky side.

1	5-oz/142 g tin baby clams, reserving the liquid	1
6	medium tomatoes, chopped into 8 pieces each	6
1	medium red pepper, seeded and cut into chunks	1
2 tbsp	fresh basil, chopped	25 mL
1 tbsp	olive oil	15 mL
1 tbsp	balsamic vinegar	15 mL
1/4 cup	dry white wine	50 mL
1	large potato, cut into cubes	1
1	medium carrot, diced	1
	Salt	
	Fresh ground black pepper	

Preheat oven to 375°F/ 190°C.

In a medium-size bowl toss the tomatoes and peppers with the basil, olive oil and balsamic vinegar. Turn into a medium-size casserole, cover tightly with a lid or foil and roast in the oven for 30 minutes until the tomatoes and peppers are mushy.

Meanwhile, drain the reserved clam juice into a medium saucepan.

Add the wine, potato and carrot. Bring to a boil, reduce heat and simmer for 10 to 15 minutes or until the potato is tender.

Combine the cooked potato, carrot and liquid with the roasted tomato and pepper mixture. Add clams, warm through and season to taste with salt and pepper.

Serves 2 to 3

CORNBREAD AND CLAM SCALLOP

THIS recipe was created out of stuff that just happened to be sitting in my refrigerator. Considering that I more or less threw everything together, I was especially pleased at how well it turned out. I discovered that this dish goes particularly well with steamed spinach and cauliflower.

1	5-oz/142 g tin baby clams, drained	1
3	green onions, sliced	3
1 tbsp	butter, melted	15 mL
1/4 cup	cilantro, chopped	50 mL
1 cup	cornbread crumbs	250 mL
3/4 cup	heavy cream	175 mL
1/2 cup	grated Cheddar cheese	125 mL
	Fresh ground black pepper	

Preheat oven to 350°F/180°C.

Butter a medium-size casserole dish and set aside. In a small bowl, place the clams, green onions, melted butter, cilantro and cornbread crumbs. Toss to combine. Place in the buttered casserole.

Pour the cream over the mixture evenly. Top with grated Cheddar cheese and black pepper. Cook for 15 to 20 minutes until lightly browned and bubbly.

Serves 2 to 3

Clam digging jackpot!

In 1956 the largest

clam on record was

found in Okinawa,

Japan. It weighed

340 kg (750 lb).

CRABMEAT

PART OF THE CHALLENGE with fresh crab is that you have to earn that wonderful taste by cracking the shell and picking away with tools that take the skill of an experienced locksmith. Your patience is ultimately rewarded but it can be a very frustrating experience when you taste more shell than crab. In North America the most commonly consumed crabs are the Alaskan king, snow, Dungeness, Jonah, stone, blue and soft-shell crabs. The Alaskan king crab, marketed fresh, frozen or canned, is the largest edible crab of the North Pacific, weighing up to 11 kg (25 lb) and producing at least 3 kg (6 lb) of meat. You can buy fresh, shelled crabmeat at your local fishmonger's for a king's ransom or you can head down to the supermarket and buy a tin of good quality crabmeat.

As a rule, most crabmeat is canned in its own juices and, due to its natural low fat content, is lower in calories than salmon and tuna. The recipes that I have collected for this section allow you to enjoy the genuine taste of crab without all the fuss.

CRAB RISOTTO

I was taught that it's taboo to put cheese with shellfish, but risotto is not quite the same without a little Parmesan. Some people think that you have to be over 40 to make good risotto because it takes patience. But the time you lavish on this dish is worth it.

1	4-oz/113 g tin crabmeat, drained	1
1¹/₂ cups	vegetable stock	375 mL
1 tbsp	olive oil	15 mL
1	small yellow onion, grated	1
2	cloves garlic, grated	2
³/₄ cup	arborio rice	175 mL
1 tsp	lemon juice	5 mL
¹/₂ cup	dry white wine	125 mL
1 tsp	lemon zest, grated	5 mL
1 tbsp	butter	15 mL
¹/₂ cup	Parmesan cheese	15 mL
	Fresh ground black pepper	
	Fresh chives, chopped	

In a small saucepan, heat the vegetable stock and keep warm over low heat.

In a medium saucepan, heat the olive oil over medium heat. Add the onion and garlic and sauté for 2 minutes without browning. Add the rice and stir well, being careful not to let the rice stick to the pan. Add the lemon juice and wine, stir and let the liquid absorb the rice. Lower the heat to medium-low. For the next 15 to 20 minutes, add the warm broth in 1/4-cup/ 50 mL measures, stirring well, but not constantly. (You do not want the rice to stick to the pan at all.)

When the broth has all been incorporated, your rice should be ready. If the rice is not tender, add more wine or hot water and continue to cook.

Remove from heat, add the lemon zest, butter, cheese and crabmeat. Fold into the rice. Cover and let sit for 5 minutes.

Add pepper to taste and garnish with chopped chives.

Serves 2

CRABMEAT ON TOAST

WHEN I WAS 16, I had a summer job at the Terminal City Club in Vancouver working in the laundry. It was the toughest physical job that I have ever endured. I did, however, learn two things. One, I never wanted to do laundry ever again and, two, the favourite luncheon dish at this club was Crab Legs on Toast. Although I've never had Crab Legs on Toast at the Terminal City Club, the rave reviews inevitably inspired me to create this recipe.

1	4-oz/113 g tin crabmeat	1
¼ cup	mayonnaise	50 mL
½ tsp	lemon juice	2 mL
½	stalk celery, chopped	½
1 tbsp	green onions, chopped	15 mL
1	tomato, sliced into 8 very thin slices	1
2	slices of sourdough bread, toasted	2
	Fresh ground black pepper	

In a bowl mix together the crabmeat, mayonnaise, lemon juice, celery and green onions. Place 4 slices of tomato on each piece of toasted sourdough. Top with the crabmeat mixture and fresh ground black pepper to taste. Place under the broiler for 2 to 3 minutes until bubbly and warmed through.

Serves 1 to 2

Battle of the sexes!

During the onetime,

48-hour mating session

of the female blue crab,

she sheds her shell and

is subsequently cradled

by her male partner

until a new shell is

formed. Once this is

achieved, the male

crab must scurry for his

life or be attacked and

consumed by his un-

grateful mate.

CRAB AND GOAT CHEESE STRUDEL

WORKING WITH phyllo dough is not the easiest thing to do at first, but after a few times you will feel as if you were born on the Isle of Crete. You need to work quickly so the sheets do not crumble or crack. Phyllo dough is available in most large grocery stores and specialty markets in the freezer section.

1	4-oz/113 g tin crabmeat	1
2 tbsp	butter	25 mL
4^1/$_2$ tsp	olive oil	22 mL
7	sheets of phyllo dough	7
4 oz	fresh goat cheese, crumbled	125 g
^{1}/$_4$ cup	chopped basil	50 mL
^{1}/$_4$ cup	pine nuts, toasted	50 mL
2 tsp	dry sherry	10 mL
	Fresh ground black pepper	

Preheat oven to 375°F/180°C.

Melt the butter and olive oil together.

Lay one sheet of the phyllo dough flat on a clean dry work surface with the long edge facing you. Brush the phyllo lightly and evenly with the butter mixture. Lay a second sheet of phyllo directly on top of the buttered one. Butter this one and repeat the process until you have buttered and layered all the phyllo sheets.

Lay the crabmeat on the edge of the phyllo, about 2 inches/5 cm from the bottom edge and about 1 inch/2.5 cm from each side. Cover the crabmeat with the crumbled goat cheese, basil and pine nuts. Sprinkle with the sherry and ground black pepper.

Fold the 2-inch/5 cm flap over the filling and fold the sides over this. Roll up the strudel as tightly as possible. Brush the roll with the remaining butter mixture and place it seam-side down on an ungreased baking sheet.

Bake 20 to 25 minutes until the strudel is golden brown. Allow to cool slightly before slicing. Cut with a serrated knife into 6 to 12 pieces.

Serves 4

KENTUCKY CRAB CRÊPES

THIS IS DETIVED from a traditional dish
from the southern United States called Kentucky Hot
Browns. I first adapted the recipe for my restaurant
and now I have adapted it for a tin of crab.

1	4-oz/113 g tin crabmeat	1
1 tbsp	butter	15 mL
1 tbsp	flour	15 mL
3/4 cup	milk	175 mL
1 tsp	Worcestershire sauce (or more to your taste)	5 mL
1/2 cup	grated Cheddar cheese	125 mL
2	large crêpes (either your own recipe or frozen)	2
2	tomatoes, finely chopped	2
2	green onions, sliced	2
1	green onion, chopped	1
2 tbsp	grated Parmesan cheese	25 mL
	Fresh ground black pepper	

In a small to medium saucepan, melt the butter and add the flour, stirring together for 1 minute. Do not brown. Slowly add the milk, stirring constantly to make a medium to thick white sauce. Add the Worcestershire sauce and the Cheddar cheese and stir until well combined.

Lay your crêpes in a low flat dish. Divide the crabmeat between the two crêpes, then top with the tomatoes and sliced green onions. Place 2 tbsp/25 mL of sauce on each, then fold the crêpes over. Top each crêpe with the rest of the sauce and place under the broiler for a minute or so, until bubbly and warmed through.

Place the crêpes on your serving dish and garnish with chopped green onion, Parmesan cheese and fresh ground pepper.

Serves 2

CREAMED CURRIED CRAB AND SHRIMP

EITHER YOU LIKE curry or you don't. I grew up on curried shrimp and there's no question that I like it. Even if you think you don't, try this simple dish. It is so good that it may change your inclinations.

1	4-oz/113 g tin crabmeat	1
1	4-oz/113 g tin shrimp	1
1 1/2 tsp	butter	7 mL
1 1/2 tsp	olive oil	7 mL
1	small onion, grated	1
2	cloves garlic, grated	2
1 tbsp	curry powder	15 mL
1 tsp	tomato paste	5 mL
1/4 cup	dry white wine	50 mL
1 cup	heavy cream	250 mL
3 cups	cooked hot rice, basmati or plain	750 mL
	Raisins, chopped green onion, plain yogourt (if desired for garnish)	

> The seal of a can was
> originally tested with a
> sharp whack of a wooden
> mallet. A clear sound
> indicated a proper seal,
> a dull one revealed an
> improper closure.

In a medium-size saucepan over medium heat, melt the butter and olive oil together and add the onion. Sauté for 1 minute until almost translucent.
Add the garlic and curry powder, stirring constantly to prevent burning.
Add the tomato paste, stir well and cook for another ¹/₂ minute.

Stir in the wine and cook to reduce most of the liquid away. Add the cream and bring to a boil. Reduce heat and simmer until the mixture thickens slightly.

Add the shrimp and crabmeat, heat through and serve over the hot rice.
Garnish as desired.

Serves 2

CRAB AND POLENTA BAKE WITH SUN-DRIED TOMATO AND PESTO

SOME WOULD argue that Italian home cooking is as good as, if not better than, the elegant dishes in the best Italian restaurants. That's because any Italian restaurant dish owes a sizable debt to the kitchens of Mamas all over Italy. This dish is inspired by everything I love about Italian food.

2	4-oz/125 g tins crabmeat, drained	2
¹/₂ cup	cream	125 mL
¹/₄ cup	pesto sauce	50 mL
4	pieces sun-dried tomatoes, sliced	4
2 tbsp	pine nuts, toasted	25 mL
2	green onions, sliced	2
3 cups	water	750 mL
1 cup	yellow cornmeal	250 mL
1	egg	1
1 tbsp	butter	15 mL
¹/₂ cup	Parmesan cheese, grated, plus 2 tbsp/25 mL for topping	125 mL

Preheat oven to 350°F/180°C. Butter a medium-size casserole dish.

Mix the cream and pesto together in a small saucepan over medium heat. Cook for a few minutes to reduce slightly. Add the sun-dried tomatoes, pine nuts, onions and crabmeat. Place this mixture in the casserole dish.

In a medium-size, heavy-bottomed saucepan, bring the water to a boil. Lower the heat and slowly add the cornmeal stirring until smooth and thick, about 5 minutes. Remove from heat and add the egg, butter and cheese. Mix well and pour onto the crab mixture in the casserole dish. Sprinkle with the 2 tbsp/25 mL Parmesan cheese.

Bake for 20 to 30 minutes until brown and bubbly.

Serves 2 to 3

CRABCAKES WITH CAYENNE MAYONNAISE

WHEN I HAD my restaurant, this was my signature dish. And like all signature dishes, it has a classic combination of flavours and textures that contribute to its lasting popularity. People used to come from miles around for this one.

3	4-oz/113 g tins crabmeat, drained	3
2 tbsp	tomato paste	25 mL
1/4 tsp	cayenne pepper	1 mL
1 tsp	lemon juice	5 mL
2	green onions, finely chopped	2
1 tbsp	fresh cilantro, finely chopped	15 mL
1	egg, lightly beaten	1
2 tbsp	grated Parmesan cheese	25 mL
3 tbsp	cornmeal, divided	45 mL
1 tbsp	butter	15 mL
1 tbsp	olive oil	15 mL

Mayonnaise:

1/4 cup	mayonnaise	50 mL
1/2 tsp	cayenne pepper	2 mL
	Lemon wedges	

Place crabmeat in a bowl with next seven ingredients and 1 tbsp/15 mL of cornmeal. Mix until well combined and form into 4 patties. Dredge patties in remaining 2 tbsp/25 mL cornmeal.

In a fry pan, melt butter and olive oil together over medium-high heat until bubbling. Turn heat down to medium and place patties in the pan. Use a spatula to flatten the patties a bit. Cook for 3 to 5 minutes on each side. Crabcakes should be nicely browned and cooked through.

Mix mayonnaise and cayenne pepper together and serve on the side of the crabcakes with the lemon wedges.

Serves 2

SHIITAKE MUSHROOMS STUFFED WITH CRABMEAT

sometimes one specific ingredient makes an entire dish. In this case, adjusting the amount of wasabi mustard to your taste raises this recipe well above the ordinary.

1	4-oz/113 g tin crabmeat, drained	1
1 1/2 tsp	butter	7 mL
3	green onions, finely chopped	3
16 to 18	shiitake mushrooms about 2 inches/5 cm in size, stems removed (finely chop two of the caps and reserve)	16 to 18
2 tbsp	mirin	25 mL
3/4 cup	heavy cream	175 mL
1/4 tsp	wasabi mustard (or to taste)	1 mL
1/2 cup	bread crumbs	125 mL
1/4 cup	grated Parmesan cheese	50 mL
	Fresh ground black pepper	

In a medium-size saucepan over medium heat, melt the butter and add the green onions and the chopped mushroom caps. Sauté for a minute or two until softened. Add the mirin, reduce for a few seconds, then add the heavy cream. Reduce until cream reaches a thick consistency.

Remove from heat and fold in the wasabi mustard, crabmeat and bread crumbs. Taste, and add more wasabi mustard if you wish it to be hotter. Combine well.

Divide mixture between the mushroom caps, approximately 1 tbsp/5 mL per mushroom. Sprinkle the Parmesan cheese on top of the mushrooms and grind fresh black pepper on top.

Place under the broiler for 3 to 4 minutes until brown and bubbly. Be careful not to burn.

Serves 4 as an appetizer

The giant spider crab of Japan is the largest living crustacean, with legs that often exceed 120 cm (4 ft) and a shell width of 30 cm (1 ft) or more.

CRAB AND SPAGHETTI SQUASH WITH LEMON BUTTER

MANY PEOPLE are intimidated by the mere mention of spaghetti squash. It strikes them as hopelessly exotic and, consequently, they don't cook with it. Here's an easy way to enjoy this unfairly neglected squash and impress yourself at the same time.

1	4-oz/113 g tin crabmeat, drained	1
1	medium-size spaghetti squash	1
2 tbsp	butter	25 mL
2 tbsp	olive oil	25 mL
1	clove garlic, finely chopped	1
2 tbsp	parsley, chopped	25 mL
2 tbsp	chives, chopped	25 mL
1/2 cup	dry white wine	125 mL
	Zest of 1 lemon	
	Juice of 1 lemon	
1/2 cup	cashew pieces or pine nuts, toasted	125 mL
	Salt	
	Fresh ground black pepper	

Preheat oven to 400°F/200°C.

Cut squash in half lengthwise and scoop out seeds. Place cut side down on baking tray with ½ cup/125 mL water. Bake for 30 minutes or until the strands will separate. Remove from oven and cool. With a fork, separate strands and place in a bowl.

In a medium to large fry pan, melt the butter and olive oil until bubbly. Add the garlic and sauté for 1 minute. Add 3 cups of spaghetti squash, parsley and chives. Add white wine, lemon zest and lemon juice and cook for 1 minute. Add crabmeat and nuts and warm through for 2 to 3 minutes. Season with salt and pepper.

Serves 3 to 4

BUTTERNUT SQUASH AND CRAB SOUP

THIS SOUP IS quick to make and low in fat, but it doesn't taste like it. The addition of crabmeat adds a special richness. And, this soup is exceptionally nourishing. It's rich in fibre, which helps lower cholesterol levels, and it includes more than the recommended daily intake of beta-carotene.

1	4-oz/113 g tin crabmeat, drained	1
4 cups	vegetable stock	1 L
1	small butternut squash, peeled and cubed	1
2	small leeks, chopped	2
1/4 tsp	grated nutmeg	50 mL
	Fresh ground black pepper	
	Pinch salt	
	Sprigs of watercress	

In a medium to large pot, bring the vegetable stock to a boil over high heat. Add the squash and leeks, return to boil. Reduce to simmer until squash is soft (about 10 minutes).

Place the mixture in a food processor and purée. Add the nutmeg, salt and pepper to taste. Fold in crabmeat and place in serving bowls. Garnish with the sprigs of watercress.

Serves 2 to 3

CRAB LOUIS SANDWICH

WHEN I MAKE a sandwich I rarely put butter or mayonnaise on the bread. With this recipe, the mayonnaise in the mixture is satisfying enough.

1	4-oz/113 g tin crabmeat, drained	1
2 tbsp	mayonnaise	25 mL
1 tbsp	cocktail sauce	15 mL
1	hard-boiled egg, chopped	1
1/2	avocado, chopped	1/2
1	plum tomato, chopped	1
3	sun-dried black olives, pitted and chopped	3
1 tbsp	fresh basil, chopped	45 mL
	Fresh ground black pepper	
8	slices sourdough bread	8
8	arugula leaves, chopped	8
1 cup	iceberg lettuce, shredded	250 mL

In a medium-size bowl, whisk together the mayonnaise and cocktail sauce. Add the crabmeat, egg,
avocado, plum tomato, olives and basil. Fold gently
until all ingredients are well combined. Season
with the fresh ground black pepper to taste.

Lay out 4 slices of the bread, divide mixture
among the slices and top with the arugula and
shredded lettuce. Cover each with another slice
and cut each sandwich in two.

Serves 4

In classic medieval
excess, the banquet
presented to Elizabeth of
Austria when she made
her ceremonial entrance
to Paris in 1571 consist-
ed, *in part,* of four large
salmon, 10 large turbot,
50 crabs, 18 trout,
17 pike, three baskets
of large smelts, three
baskets of oysters, one
basket of mussels, 400
herrings, 12 lobsters, 50
pounds of whale, 200
cod tripes, 12 carp and
1,000 frogs.

Pacific Pearl
BRAND
CONTENTS 10 OZ. AV.
WASH. CERT. NO. 262
WILLAPA BAY
FROZEN FRESH
OYSTERS

OYSTERS

You DON'T HAVE TO be a Rockefeller to celebrate the oyster in its
many different forms. Oysters in the tin are not for slurping raw with champagne or vodka. But you may be surprised at just how versatile tinned oysters
can be. Most of us are aware of how popular smoked oysters are at a cocktail
party. And it's hard to resist oysters, either fresh or tinned, when you fry them
up with a well-seasoned coating in butter or, for reduced cholesterol, olive oil.
Beyond these well-known recipes, tinned oysters have a substance that make
for a welcome variation from more traditional stews and pot pies.

There was a time when oysters were eaten only in those months possess-
ing the letter r. Oysters harvested in the months of May, June, July and August
were considered unhealthy and even poisonous. This custom was no doubt
due to the challenge of keeping oysters cool in warmer weather and the fact
that they tend to be thin, watery and less flavourful in the summer months.
Today oysters can be enjoyed year-round, especially if you harvest them from
a tin.

SEARED OYSTERS WITH SPINACH AND BACON

THanks To the addition of bacon, which stands up to oysters extremely well, this qualifies as one of my favourite recipes. Definitely a sensual pleasure.

1	5-oz/142 g tin oysters, drained	1
1/4 lb	bacon	125 g
1	bunch fresh spinach	1
1	clove garlic, chopped	1
2 tbsp	soy sauce	25 mL
1 tbsp	sesame oil	15 mL
1 tbsp	olive oil	15 mL
2 tbsp	sesame seeds, toasted	25 mL

Dice bacon into small pieces, fry over medium heat until crisp and pour off fat except for 1 tbsp/15 mL. Remove bacon from pan and set aside.

Steam spinach until just limp (undercooked).

Add garlic to the reserved bacon fat in fry pan. Stir, but do not brown. Add spinach, soy sauce and sesame oil. Cook for 1 minute to combine flavours, remove from pan and set aside.

Return pan to high heat and add olive oil. When smoking, sear oysters until brown on both sides. Add bacon.

Lift out the spinach from its juices and place in the centre of your serving plate. Place seared oysters and bacon on top and drizzle cooking juices over all. Sprinkle toasted sesame seeds on top and serve with lemon wedges.

Serves 2

"He was a bold man that first ate an oyster."

— Jonathan Swift

PAN-FRIED OYSTERS

THe FIrST TIMe I had oysters, when I was very young, my mother pan-fried them. I can still taste them now. When I owned a restaurant, we changed my mother's version to Oysters Pan-Fried with Blue Cornmeal and Sun-Dried Tomato Salsa. This recipe is a combination of both these two variations.

1	5-oz/142 g tin oysters, drained	1
3/4 cup	blue cornmeal	175 mL
1/4 cup	grated Parmesan cheese	50 mL
1	egg	1
1 tsp	milk	5 mL
	Dash cayenne pepper (or to taste)	
2 tbsp	butter, melted	25 mL
2 tbsp	olive oil	25 mL
	Fresh parsley or basil	
	Lemon wedges	
	Flavoured mayonnaise	

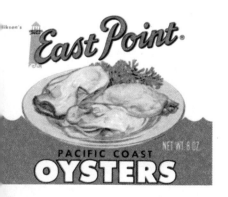

In a medium-size bowl, combine the cornmeal and the Parmesan cheese.

In a small bowl, lightly beat the egg, milk and cayenne pepper together.

Over medium heat in large fry pan, heat the butter and olive oil until bubbling. Taking one oyster at a time, coat with the egg mixture, then with the cornmeal mixture. Place in the bubbling butter and fry for 30 to 40 seconds per side.

Place cooked oysters on paper towels, then arrange on your serving platter. Garnish with fresh parsley or basil. Serve with lemon wedges or your favourite flavour of mayonnaise such as garlic, chive or sun-dried tomato!

Serves 2 as a main course

Oysters are renowned as a great aphrodisiac. Legend has it that Casanova, the celebrated Italian lover, ate 50 raw oysters every day before breakfast.

SMOKED OYSTER SPREAD

smoked oysters on their own are a delight. Many late night snacks in my home have consisted of opening a tin and devouring the morsels in no time. This more sophisticated recipe can be prepared ahead and served in hollowed-out cherry tomatoes, or it can be frozen and served hot on whatever bread product you have handy. I like to use toasted French bread rounds.

1	5-oz/142 g tin smoked oysters, drained	1
5 oz	cream cheese	142 g
1 1/2 tsp	lemon juice	7 mL
1 tsp	light cream	5 mL
1/2 tsp	onion, minced	2 mL
1/2 tsp	garlic, minced	2 mL
	Dash Worcestershire sauce	
	French bread rounds	

Place all ingredients in a food processor and pulse
a few times until well combined, but not mushy.

Using a teaspoon, place 1-inch/2.5 cm
mounds of the mixture onto a baking sheet and
place sheet in the freezer. Freeze until firm and store in airtight containers.

When you are ready to serve this delight, place the mounds on toasted
French bread rounds. Bake at 375°F/190°C for 10 minutes.

Makes 16 rounds

CHRISTMAS EVE OYSTERS

CHRISTMAS EVE IS my favourite day of the season. It is when I like to cook turkey dinner, with a southern flair, for friends and family. Since I have an abiding passion for this regional cooking, oysters are a very special part of this very special dinner.

1	5-oz/142 g tin oysters drained, reserving liquid	1
½ cup	rosé wine	125 mL
2	shallots, sliced into thin rings	2
½ cup	bread crumbs	125 mL
1 tsp	garlic, chopped	5 mL
¼ tsp	cumin	1 mL
1 tbsp	parsley, chopped	15 mL

In a fry pan, combine the rosé wine and the oyster liquid over medium to high heat. Reduce for a few minutes, then add the shallots and cook for 1 minute. Add the oysters and cook together for about 1 minute. Remove from heat. If your pan is not suitable to put in the oven, place mixture in a shallow casserole dish. There should be about $^1/_4$ cup/50 mL of liquid left to cover the oysters.

In a food processor combine the bread crumbs, garlic, cumin and parsley. Cover the oysters with this mixture and place under the broiler for about 1 to 2 minutes. Be careful not to burn.

Serves 4 as an appetizer, or 8 as a taster before a dinner

In ancient Greece votes were cast by marking one's choice on the inside of an oyster shell.

ROQUEFORT AND RED PEPPER BAKED OYSTERS

THE NEAT THING about this recipe is that you can make up the Roquefort mixture ahead of time and keep it in the freezer. This savoury butter is good on steaks, chicken or pork but unforgettable on oysters. Roquefort cheese matches the power of the oyster bite for bite.

1	5-oz/142 g tin oysters, drained	1
1/4 cup	red pepper, chopped	50 mL
4 oz	Roquefort cheese	125 g
4 oz	butter	125 g
2	cloves garlic	2
1 tbsp	parsley, chopped	15 mL
2 tbsp	bread crumbs	25 mL
	Fresh ground black pepper	

Divide the oysters among 4 small ovenproof dishes such as coquille shells.

In a food processor combine the red pepper, cheese, butter and garlic. Spoon the butter mixture onto a piece of wax paper and roll into a cylinder about 2 inches/5 cm wide.

For each dish, cut a piece of butter $^1/_2$ inch/ 1 cm and place on the oysters. (The rest of the mixture can be wrapped in plastic wrap and frozen for other uses.)

Combine the parsley and bread crumbs and sprinkle over each dish. Grind black pepper on top and place under the broiler for 3 to 5 minutes or until brown and bubbly.

Serves 4 as an appetizer

It is rumoured that Napoleon's military successes were due in part to his habit of dining on oysters before every battle.

OYSTER POT PIE

I have always found any kind of pot pie to be comforting, but the oysters in this recipe add a distinctly sensual flavour. I have served this with great success using a sweet potato crust, but you may use your favourite savoury pastry recipe for tantalizing results.

1	5-oz/142 g tin oysters, drained	1
1 tbsp	butter	15 mL
1 tbsp	flour	15 mL
3/4 cup	milk	175 mL
2 strips	bacon, cut into 1/2-inch/1 cm pieces	2
1	stock celery, diced	1
1	medium carrot, diced	1
1/2 cup	oysters mushrooms	125 mL
1/4 cup	dry white wine	50 mL
1/2 cup	green onions, sliced (both the white and green of the onion)	125 mL
	Pastry to cover a 6-inch/15 cm soufflé dish	
1	egg beaten with 1/2 tsp/2 mL water, for egg wash	1

Preheat oven to 350°F/180°C.

In a small saucepan, melt butter and add the
flour to make a roux. Slowly add the milk until you
have a white sauce that is not too thick. Remove
from heat and set aside.

In a small fry pan over medium heat, fry the bacon until cooked, but not
crispy. Add the celery, carrot and oyster mushrooms and cook for 2 minutes.
Add the wine, reduce a little, then add the onions. Combine this mixture with
the white sauce.

Place the oysters in the soufflé dish, pour the sauce over the oysters and
fold the entire mixture together.

Roll the pastry to $1/8$-inch/3 mm thickness. Place over the filling, pressing
the pastry to the edges of the dish to seal. Brush the pastry with the egg wash,
poke the pastry with a fork about 6 times and place the soufflé dish on a baking
sheet. Bake for 30 minutes or until the crust is golden brown.

Serves 2

OYSTER AND ARTICHOKE STEW

THIS IS a rich dish with a sinfully high decadence factor. I used to serve this creation at my restaurant and would lick out the pan after every serving! This stew works well as a main course with multi-grain bread and a green salad.

1	5-oz/142 g tin oysters, drained	1
1/4 cup	dry white wine	50 mL
	Pinch cayenne pepper	
1 1/2 cups	heavy cream	275 mL
1	14-oz /398 mL tin artichokes in water, drained and cut into quarters	1
1/4 cup	grated Parmesan cheese	50 mL
2	green onions, sliced	2
	Fresh ground black pepper	

Pearls of any worth

are rarely generated

by North American

oysters, which seem

only to create dull,

malformed lumps

that resemble wads of

used chewing gum.

In a medium-size saucepan over medium to high heat, combine the wine, cayenne pepper and cream. Reduce by a third. Add the artichokes and the oysters. (You may not want to add all the artichokes; the amount is just my personal preference.) Warm through for a few minutes. When mixture is at a medium thickness, remove from heat and divide between 2 bowls and top with the Parmesan cheese, the sliced green onions and the black pepper.

Serves 2

SALMON

For me, there are few things more tempting than gently easing a fork into a savoury chunk of tinned salmon. For such a simple gesture, it is filled with mouth-watering expectation, releasing several subtly different flavours at once. Maybe that's why salmon, more than any other fish I can think of, tastes of the sea. And – just like the sea – it's subject to change at a moment's notice. At first delicate, and then suddenly emphatic as you roll it on your tongue. Still, if you can hold back on the excitement of purchasing a tin, it's wise to read the label to find out the species and nutritional content of the fish inside.

Chinook, the fattiest and most intense in colour of all salmon, boasts the highest content of omega-3 fatty acids. Omega-3, a polyunsaturated fat found in the flesh of fish, has been credited with playing a preventative role in cardiovascu-lar disease and with the lowering of triglycerides. Many studies boast the health-promoting qualities that this desirable fat offers, such as lowering of cholesterol and aiding in the control of inflammatory responses in the body that cause arthritis and psoriasis. The dense and velvety sockeye and the practical pink are the two species you will see most often in your supermarket, with sockeye, the "caviar" of tinned salmon, being the most versatile. These two varieties, although lighter in fat content than chinook, have a richly lingering flavour and are well suited to hot or cold recipes using herbs and vegetables. When cooking with pink salmon I always add a little more of whatever I am using to enhance the recipe. Pink salmon's lean-er nature makes it less succulent and full-bodied than the elegant sockeye, but it's still a wonderful product.

When you open a tin of salmon you will see that the skin and bones have been processed with the fish. Many people choose to remove these; some processors are even canning their fish boneless and skinless for the convenience of the consumer. I personally love the bones and eat them as a reward for successfully opening the tin. The sensuous crunch is an acquired taste, but the bones can be easily crushed into translucent pieces. Not only is this part of the fish a rich source of calcium, much needed for the prevention of osteoporosis, but its slight crunchiness also adds texture to a recipe.

But quite apart from this useful information, the most important aspect of salmon, I think, is that it is the most exciting of all tinned fish.

SALMON AND BEAN
IN A BAGUETTE

An inventive Argentine friend gave me the idea
for this recipe. Raised on beef, he came to the joys of
tin fish late in life. Being a fervent convert, he is always
looking for ways to eat healthier with satisfying results.
This is one of his favourite lunches. The beans add a
protein boost to an already protein-rich recipe.

1	7.5-oz/213 g tin sockeye salmon, drained	1
1/2	14-oz/398 mL tin red kidney beans, drained (reserve the liquid)	1/2
1	baguette	1
1	small stock celery, finely diced	1
1	green onion, sliced	1
1 tbsp	fresh parsley, chopped	15 mL
1 tbsp	lemon juice	15 mL
	Fresh ground pepper	

Drain the salmon and kidney beans. (Reserve the remaining kidney beans in their juice for another use.) Cut the baguette into 2 or 3 pieces and hollow them out. In a bowl, combine salmon, kidney beans, celery, green onion, parsley, lemon juice and pepper to taste. Stuff the baguettes with the mixture.

Serves 2 to 3

The word *salmon* comes

from the Latin verb

salio, to leap. It is

believed that the name

sockeye derives from

the Native *Sau-kai,*

meaning chief of fishes.

SUSAN'S SALMON BURGERS

susan is an English friend of mine who, among her many attributes, can boast being a wonderful cook. This is a convenient recipe she developed for her busy family. Not only is it easy to prepare in the manner of a classic burger, but it also has strong appeal for all ages.

Salmon burgers are a healthy option for beef burgers, containing only one-third the saturated fat of the moo-based variety.

2	7.5-oz/213 g (or 1 15-oz/425 g) tin salmon, drained and flaked	2
1	egg, slightly beaten	1
1/2 cup	onion, diced	125 mL
1/2 cup	green pepper, finely chopped	125 mL
1/2 cup	fresh whole wheat bread crumbs	125 mL
1 tbsp	lemon juice	15 mL
1 tsp	(or more) lemon peel, grated	5 mL
1/2 tsp	dried rosemary, crushed	2 mL
	Fresh ground black pepper	
1 tbsp	oil	15 mL

Combine all of the ingredients except oil and mix well. Form into 4 or 5 patties.

Heat oil in fry pan and cook patties until lightly browned on each side. Serve on toasted hamburger buns with your favourite toppings (e.g., lettuce, tomato, etc.).

Serves 4

The first mechanization of salmon canning occurred in 1906 with a daunting-looking machine that beheaded, gutted and washed the fish in rapid succession.

SALMON AND FENNEL STEW

when I worked for fabled restaurateur Umberto Menghi, many moons ago, we used to serve a unique entrée with fresh salmon and fennel. This is a different recipe that has all the comforting qualities of a faithful stew, but retains the tempting combination of flavours.

1	7.5-oz/213 g tin salmon, drained	1
1 tbsp	butter	15 mL
1 1/2 tsp	olive oil	7 mL
1	clove garlic, sliced	1
1	small bulb fennel, sliced (reserve ferns for garnish)	1
1	small red pepper, cut into chunks	1
4	small tomatoes, cut into quarters	4
2	green onions, sliced	2
30	leaves spinach	30
	Fresh ground black pepper	

Place a saucepan over medium heat. Melt butter and olive oil together. Put sliced garlic and fennel in the pan. Soften for $^1/_2$ minute. Add red pepper and tomatoes. Cover, lower heat and simmer for 10 minutes. When mixture is soft and flavourful, remove from heat and add green onions, spinach and chunks of salmon. Put back on element and heat thoroughly for about 1 to 2 minutes. Add ground pepper to taste.

Garnish with fennel.

Serves 2 to 3

SALMON AND CHEDDAR QUICHE

THIS DISH IS based on one of the first recipes that I, as a beginning cook, ever made with tinned salmon. At the time I thought it was a terribly sophisticated way to entertain. Whenever I make this I remember cooking it for my girlfriends and feeling very "continental."

1	7.5-oz/213 g tin salmon, drained and flaked	1
1	9-inch/23 cm pastry shell	1
1 cup	Cheddar cheese, grated	250 mL
1/4 cup	green onions, sliced	50 mL
5	leaves fresh basil, sliced (or 1/2 tsp/2 mL dried)	5
2 tbsp	pimento, chopped	25 mL
2	large eggs	2
1 cup	light cream	250 mL
1/4 cup	grated Parmesan cheese	50 mL
	Fresh ground black pepper	

Preheat oven to 375°F/190°C. Place rack in the middle of the oven.

Bake the pastry shell for 10 minutes. Remove shell from the oven and lower heat to 350°F/180°C.

Distribute salmon on the pastry shell. Cover with Cheddar cheese, onions, basil and pimento.

Beat eggs well with cream and pepper. Pour over salmon mixture and sprinkle with Parmesan cheese. Bake for 40 minutes.

Allow to sit for a moment before you slice and serve.

Serves 4

While Pacific salmon

die after spawning

once, some Atlantic

salmon are able to

spawn several times

in a lifetime.

CURRIED SALMON LOAF

I Grew up with a basic salmon loaf that my Granny
called her own. She was an English cook and it was a
staple of her recipe files. It continues to remind me of
her and I love the memory, but I had to create my own
version to satisfy my spicier palate.

1	7.5-oz/213 g tin salmon, drained	1
1 tbsp	butter	15 mL
1 ¹/₂ tsp	curry powder	7 mL
1	large green onion, sliced	1
1	medium tomato, finely chopped	1
1	small carrot, grated	1
1	small parsnip, grated	1
1	egg	1
¹/₄ cup	grated Parmesan cheese	50 mL
2	lemon wedges	2

Heat oven to 350°F/180°C. Place the rack in the middle of the oven.

Butter an 8-inch/20 cm loaf pan with 1 tsp/5 mL butter.

Put salmon in a bowl and set aside. Melt butter in a small saucepan over medium heat. Add curry powder and cook for ½ minute, being careful not to let the mixture burn! Add green onion, tomato, carrot and parsnip and stir. Turn heat down to medium-low and cover the saucepan. Cook for 2 minutes, being careful not to let it brown.

Remove from heat and add to salmon in bowl. Add egg and Parmesan cheese. Mix well, but not into a mush. Place in loaf pan and cook in oven, covered, for 35 minutes. Remove lid and cook for 2 more minutes.

Garnish with lemon wedges.

Serves 2

SWISS CHARD AND SALMON LASAGNA

THIS recipe IS somewhat fussy, but it will be sure to impress your most discriminating guests. To add a more dramatic flare to this dish, use the heartier shiitake mushroom. For increased richness that is impossible for the true gourmet to resist, you can use heavy cream instead of milk for the béchamel sauce.

1	7.5-oz/213 g tin salmon, drained	1
6	large chard leaves	6
1 1/2 cups	ricotta cheese	375 mL
1/2 cup	grated Parmesan cheese, divided	125 mL
1	egg	1
1 tbsp	olive oil	15 mL
2	cloves garlic, sliced	2
1/2 lb	mushrooms, sliced	250 g
2	green onions, sliced	2

Béchamel Sauce:

1 tbsp	butter	15 mL
1 tbsp	flour	15 mL
1 1/3 cup	milk	325 mL

To make béchamel sauce, melt butter over medium to low heat. Add flour and stir with wooden spoon for 1 minute. Be careful not to allow the mixture to burn. Add milk slowly, stirring constantly until the sauce is thick. Remove from heat.

Preheat oven to 350°F/180°C. Place the rack in the middle of the oven.

Steam the chard leaves (or place in boiling water) for 30 seconds. Set aside.

In a bowl, mix together the ricotta cheese, 1/3 cup/75 mL of the Parmesan cheese and the egg. Set aside.

Heat the olive oil in a fry pan over medium heat. Add the garlic, mushrooms and green onions. Sauté gently for 3 to 5 minutes or until the mushrooms are limp.

Line the bottom of an 11-inch/28 cm casserole with 1/3 of the béchamel sauce. Place 2 of the chard leaves on top. Place half the mushroom mixture on the chard, then half the tin of salmon on the mushrooms. Pour half the ricotta mixture on the salmon and cover with 2 more chard leaves, the remaining mushroom mixture, the salmon, the ricotta and the last 2 chard leaves. Cover the entire mixture with the remaining béchamel and sprinkle with the remaining Parmesan cheese.

Bake 40 minutes. Remove and let it sit for a moment before cutting into portions.

Serves 4

SALMON TAMALE PIE

I LOVE the texture of a cornmeal crust, which is why I am so attracted to Tamale Pie. I just had to make it with salmon.

1	7.5-oz/213 g tin salmon	1
1 tbsp	vegetable oil	15 mL
1	clove garlic, sliced	1
1/3 cup	celery, sliced	75 mL
1/3 cup	red pepper, sliced	75 mL
1/3 cup	green onion, sliced	75 mL
1	14-oz/398 mL tin plum tomatoes	1
1 tbsp	tomato paste	15 mL
1 tsp	chili powder	5 mL
1/2 tsp	cumin powder	2 mL
1/4 tsp	paprika	1 mL
1/4 tsp	dried thyme	1 mL
1/2 cup	kernel corn	125 mL

Crust:

1 cup	milk	250 mL
3/4 cup	cornmeal	175 mL
3/4 cup	grated Cheddar cheese	175 mL
1 tbsp	green onion, chopped	15 mL

Preheat oven to 350°F/180°C. Place rack in the middle of the oven.

Heat oil in saucepan over medium heat. Add garlic, celery, red pepper and green onion. Sauté for 30 seconds. Add the tin of tomatoes, tomato paste and spices and sauté for 2 to 3 minutes. Fold in corn and salmon. Place in a 9-inch/23 cm casserole dish and set aside.

To make crust, heat milk in saucepan over medium heat. Slowly add cornmeal and stir until it has reached a creamy consistency. Add Cheddar cheese and onions. Mix together and spread over the salmon mixture.

Cook for 20 minutes or until crust is golden.

Serves 2 to 3

CORN AND
SALMON FRITTERS

THIS IS a traditional Southern recipe that becomes
a substantial appetizer with the addition of salmon. Add
a salad and you've got a delicious meal. Be careful not
to overcook it or you'll lose the wonderful melt-in-
your-mouth sensation that makes this dish so terrific.

1	3.75-oz/106 g tin salmon, drained	1
1 1/2 tsp	sugar	7 mL
1 tsp	baking powder	5 mL
1/2 tsp	baking soda	2 mL
1 cup	all-purpose flour	250 mL
3/4 cup	milk	175 mL
2 tbsp	butter, melted	25 mL
2	eggs	2
2 tbsp	red pepper, diced	25 mL
2 tbsp	celery, diced	25 mL
1	green onion, sliced	1
1/4 cup	kernel corn	50 mL
1/4 cup	grated Cheddar cheese	50 mL
	Vegetable oil	

Stir together the sugar, baking powder, baking soda and flour in a large bowl. Set aside. Stir together the milk, butter and eggs. Add to the dry ingredients in a thin and steady stream. Mix with a rubber spatula to gently fold the batter together. Do not overmix. Add the red pepper, celery, green onion, corn, salmon and Cheddar cheese. Fold together (the batter will be lumpy).

Heat $^1/_2$-inch/1 cm oil in a large skillet until a small bit of batter dropped into the oil bubbles (about 375°F/190°C). Using a $^1/_4$ cup/50 mL measure filled to $^3/_4$ full, drop batter into the oil. Fry until golden brown, about 2 minutes per side. Drain on paper towels for about 2 minutes.

Serves 2 to 3

Salmon will swim,

without feeding, up to

4,800 km (3,000 mi)

to spawn. Some believe

that salmon return to

the exact spot where

they hatched via their

sense of smell.

SALMON AND
POTATO SALAD

POTATO SALAD comes in many appetizing variations, and I love them all. And, with the welcome
addition of salmon, it becomes my "desert island
dish." A restaurant in my neighbourhood by the name
of Farrago gave me the inspiration for this spicy recipe.

1	7.5-oz/213 g tin salmon, drained	1
½ cup	sour cream	125 mL
1 tbsp	horseradish	15 mL
1	bunch watercress, broken into sections	1
½ lb	nugget potatoes, cooked and cooled	250 g
3	green onions, sliced	3
1	stalk celery, diced	1
	Fresh ground black pepper	

Mix together the sour cream and horseradish and set aside. Line a shallow salad bowl with the water-cress.

Cut the potatoes in half and set in another bowl. Add the onions, celery and salmon to the potatoes. Toss with the sour cream mixture then transfer to your presentation bowl. Sprinkle with the fresh ground pepper and top with a sprig of watercress.

Serves 2 to 3

Freshness that lasts! According to legend, canned B.C. salmon that was shipped off to allied troops in WWI was hidden and then discovered and eaten by a new generation of troops in WWII.

AVOCADO, CHICK PEA AND SALMON SALAD

THIS summer salad proves that salmon does well on the cool side. It gives you a quick but elegant way to entertain on a steamy August night after a full day's work. All three main ingredients are rich sources of protein, making this recipe a winner for those following a high-protein diet. And don't shy away from avocados because you think they're high in fat — it's monounsaturated fat, not the cholesterol-raising type.

1	7.5-oz/213 g tin salmon, drained	1
	Butter lettuce and spinach leaves	
1 cup	canned chick peas, drained	250 mL
3	green onions, sliced	3
2	radishes, cut into thin wedges	2
¹/₄ cup	carrots, grated	50 mL
¹/₄ cup	zucchini, grated	50 mL
1	avocado, sliced into wedges	1
1	ripe tomato, sliced into wedges	1

Dressing:

1 tbsp	curry powder	15 mL
2 tbsp	apple cider vinegar	25 mL
¹/₄ cup	olive oil	50 mL

To prepare dressing, placc ingredients in a small bowl and shake together.

Place the lettuce and spinach leaves in a 10-inch/25 cm shallow bowl. Add salmon, chick peas, onions, radishes, carrots and zucchini. Arrange the avocado and tomato alternately around the perimeter of the bowl.

Re-shake your dressing and pour over all. Before serving, gently toss the salad.

Serves 2 to 4

SALMON AND
BROCCOLI CHOWDER

I CREATED THIS dish out of necessity for comfort
food on a rainy November evening. This thick chowder
could almost be classified as a stew. But soup has its
own special magic. A few contemplative spoonfuls of
this dish on a cold night may conjure up welcome
memories of one of your mother's classic creations.

1	7.5-oz/213 g tin salmon, drained and flaked	1
1 tbsp	butter	15 mL
1	small red onion, sliced into rings then cut in half	1
1 tbsp	flour	15 mL
1 tsp	fresh thyme, chopped (or $^1/_2$ tsp/2 mL dried)	5 mL
2 cups	hot milk	500 mL
1 cup	potatoes, cooked and diced	250 mL
1 cup	broccoli flowers, steamed	250 mL
$^1/_4$ cup	grated Parmesan cheese	50 mL
	Fresh chives, sliced for garnish	
	Fresh ground black pepper	

In a large saucepan over medium-high heat, melt butter until foam subsides. Turn heat down to medium and add onions. Sauté for 2 minutes, making sure not to brown.

Add flour and stir until onions are coated. Add thyme.

Slowly add the milk, stirring constantly until the mixture is thick and creamy.

Add salmon, potatoes and broccoli and heat through. Serve into bowls and sprinkle with Parmesan cheese, chives and black pepper.

Serves 2 to 3

ASPARAGUS, BRIE AND SALMON OMELETTE

MY wandering friends are always returning home with tales of fabulous meals that they have experienced on their travels. This particular idea came from a friend who extolled the many virtues of a lunch he had enjoyed on a recent visit to Manhattan. He was so enthusiastic that I created my own version.

1	3.25-oz/106 g tin salmon, drained	1
1 tbsp	butter	15 mL
4	eggs, lightly beaten with 1 tbsp/15 mL water	4
3 oz	Brie cheese, sliced thin	90 g
8	stalks asparagus, trimmed and steamed for 3 to 4 minutes	8

Over medium-high heat, melt butter in a 10 inch/ 25 cm fry pan, preferably non-stick. When the foam subsides, reduce heat to medium-low.

Place egg mixture in the pan and let sit undisturbed for 15 seconds. With rubber spatula, gently move mixture around the pan. Flake salmon over the eggs, leaving a 1-inch/2.5 cm border free around the perimeter of the omelette, then add the cheese and asparagus.

Take the spatula and fold the omelette over itself in half. You may either flip it at this time or cover with a lid for a moment or two, just long enough to set, but still be creamy inside.

Serves 2

Pacific salmon occur in an estimated 1,300 to 1,500 rivers and streams in British Columbia and have been successfully introduced into New Zealand, parts of Eurasia, the Great Lakes and South America. Today, however, almost 96% of the salmon sold in supermarkets is farm-raised.

MUSHROOM, SALMON AND SPINACH FRITTATA

SOMETIMES, YOU never know what you'll come up with until you begin to experiment with leftovers in the refrigerator. I developed this recipe one leisurely Sunday morning and was surprised to discover how well the improvised marriage of ingredients worked. Now it's a regular part of my weekend whenever I'm entertaining for brunch.

1	7.5-oz/213 g tin salmon	1
4	eggs, lightly beaten	4
1/4 cup	milk	50 mL
8 oz	potatoes, cooked and sliced	250 g
2	green onions, sliced	2
8 oz	spinach, steamed	250 g
8 oz	mushrooms, sautéed	250 g
1 cup	grated Cheddar cheese	250 mL
	Salt	
	Fresh ground black pepper	

Preheat oven to 400°F/200°C. Lightly oil a casserole dish.

Mix together eggs and milk.

In the casserole, layer your ingredients in this order while sprinkling a dash of salt and pepper between each layer: potatoes, onions, spinach, salmon, mushrooms and cheese. Cover all with egg mixture.

Bake for 20 to 30 minutes.

Serves 2 to 3

PECAN SALMON ROLL

THIS IS MY variation of a recipe that I picked up on my travels in Lunenburg, Nova Scotia. I have used this versatile recipe on numerous occasions, both for myself and for events that I have catered. People never seem to tire of the tantalizing results from this simple preparation.

1	15-oz/425 g tin salmon, drained	1
9 oz	cream cheese	250 g
2 tbsp	goat cheese (optional)	25 mL
1 tbsp	lemon juice	15 mL
1	green onion, finely chopped	1
1 tbsp	horseradish	15 mL
1/2 tsp	cayenne pepper	2 mL
1/2 cup	pecans, finely chopped	125 mL
2 tbsp	parsley, chopped fine, plus a few sprigs for garnish	25 mL

Cream together cheeses, lemon juice, green onion, horseradish and cayenne pepper. Add salmon and mix together. Refrigerate at least two hours.

Shape into a roll, about 8 x 3 inches/20 x 8 cm. Roll through the combined mixture of pecans and parsley to cover. Place on platter and garnish with parsley sprigs. Serve with sliced baguette or crackers.

For an Italian spin, substitute the onion, horseradish and cayenne with 2 tbsp (25 mL) of pesto sauce and 1 tbsp (15 mL) of sun-dried tomatoes, chopped fine, and replace the parsley with basil.

Serves 6 to 10 as an appetizer

NEW ENGLAND
SALMON CAKES

A TradITIONAl New England salmon dinner consists of salmon, peas and boiled potatoes, which often end up mashed together on the plate in a comforting swirl. This is a recipe in which my two favourite things come together: salmon cakes and New England. It's a great dish to prepare from leftovers. Served with dill mayonnaise and lemon wedges, it turns into a dish that seems brand new!

1	7.5-oz/213 g tin salmon, drained	1
1 cup	creamy mashed potatoes	250 mL
1/2 cup	fresh or freeze-dried peas (cooked)	125 mL
1	egg, lightly beaten	1
1	green onion, sliced	1
1 1/2 tsp	fresh dill or 1/2 tsp/2 mL dried dill	7 mL
	Fresh ground black pepper to taste	
	Sea salt	
2 tbsp	whole wheat flour	25 mL
1 tbsp	butter	15 mL
1 tbsp	vegetable oil	15 mL

Mix together all ingredients except flour, butter and oil. Form mixture into 4 patties, and dredge them in flour.

Over medium heat, melt oil and butter together. When foamy and bubbly, add patties and fry evenly on both sides until nicely browned, about 5 minutes per side.

Serves 2

While oil or water is added to tuna in the canning process, the liquid in canned salmon comes from the fish itself.

SALMON COULIBIAC

some recipes are treasures just because they consistently live up to their sophisticated names. Coulibiac, a hot fish pie, is an innovation of Russian cuisine with worldwide appeal. So, from St. Petersburg, Russia, to St. Petersburg, Florida, this delicious dish is almost as fun to pronounce as it is to eat.

2	7.5-oz/213 g tins salmon, drained	2
1 lb	package puff pastry	500 g
1	package Uncle Ben's Wild Rice, cooked according to directions	1
2 tbsp	parsley	25 mL
2 tbsp	dill	25 mL
3	green onions, finely chopped	3
	Zest of 1 lemon	
	Salt	
	Fresh ground black pepper	
4	eggs, hard-boiled	4
1	egg, well beaten	1

Preheat oven to 425°F/220°C.

Roll out puff pastry into 2 triangles, 6 x 10 inches/15 x 25 cm. In a large bowl combine salmon, wild rice, parsley, dill, onions, lemon zest and salt and pepper to taste.

Place one of the pastry triangles on an oiled baking sheet. Spread half the rice-salmon mixture, leaving a $^1/_2$-inch/1 cm border, and arrange the hard-boiled eggs down the centre of the rice end to end. Spread the rest of the rice mixture in an even layer over the eggs. Brush the $^1/_2$-inch /1 cm border with beaten egg. Cover with the second pastry triangle and crimp the edges to form a tight seal. Chill for one hour.

Cut four small slits in the top. Brush with beaten egg.

Bake for 10 minutes. Reduce heat to 375°F/190°C for 30 minutes until golden brown.

Serves 6

South Pacific

BRAND

California

SARDINES

WATER AND SALT ADDED

SARDINES

IF THERE IS ANY one fish that seems born to the tin, it's the sardine. In countries like Spain and Portugal, fresh sardines have long been a marketplace staple. For the rest of the world, a sardine would seem naked without the familiar tin. Part of the fun of making a toasted sardine sandwich is turning back the key of the tin to reveal all the little sardines nestled comfortably in their bed.

The true European sardine is the young pilchard – a fish belonging to the herring family. The name *sardine* is, however, applied to many small fish packed with oil or sauce in distinctive flat cans. In North America, where sardine fishing and packing are big industry, small Atlantic herring are usually substituted for the pilchard.

The following recipes provide several delicious as well as nutritious reasons for sardines to leave their tin. Sardines are a terrific source of iron and are good for you in many other ways: 100 g (about eight fish) of sardines, packed with skin and bones intact, provide 40% of the recommended daily allowance of calcium and 100% of the vitamin D that is necessary for its absorption.

I prefer to buy sardines packed in their own juice or water since sardines are higher in cholesterol and fat content than salmon or tuna. Their calorie content is drastically higher when packed in oil. Prepared appropriately, the sardine is a welcome sight for breakfast, lunch or dinner.

THREE TIN TAPENADE

your can opener works overtime on this one, but it's worth it. This flavourful Mediterranean appetizer is quick to prepare and has the added benefit of satisfying a small crowd. Served on your favourite crackers, it goes particularly well with a robust red wine.

1	3.75-oz/106 g tin sardines in water, drained	1
1	1.75-oz/50 g tin anchovy, drained and soaked in ½ cup/125 mL milk for 10 to 15 minutes	1
1	6-oz/170 g tin tuna, drained	1
1	clove garlic, coarsely chopped	1
1	small shallot, coarsely chopped	1
1 cup	pitted black olives, chopped	250 mL
¼ cup	pimento, coarsely chopped	50 mL
1 tsp	grainy Dijon mustard	5 mL
6 tbsp	olive oil	75 mL
2 tbsp	dry sherry	25 mL
2 tsp	fresh rosemary	10 mL

Place all ingredients in your food processor and blend until coarsely combined, about 30 seconds.

Place in your favourite serving bowl and garnish with a sprig of rosemary.

Serves 6 to 8 as an appetizer

The sardine is fished in great quantities off the islands of Sardinia, from which it takes its name.

SARDINE, RED ONION AND CAMBONZOLA SANDWICH

WHILE SHOPPING at a local market I bumped into Craig, a friend of mine. When I told him about this book he shared this recipe, a favourite of both Craig and his father.

1	3.75-oz/106 g tin sardines in spring water	1
2 tbsp	mayonnaise	25 mL
4	slices sourdough bread	4
2	ripe tomatoes, sliced	2
	Salt	
	Fresh ground black pepper	
2	slices red onion, cut into rings and soaked in 2 tsp/10 mL balsamic vinegar	2
4 oz	Cambonzola cheese	125 g
	Lettuce leaves, washed and dried	

Spread mayonnaise onto slices of sourdough bread. Next, layer sliced tomato, and season with salt and pepper if desired. Divide drained sardines between two sandwiches, pressing each fish slightly to flatten. Remove backbone if desired. Top with drained slices of onion, dot with chunks of cheese and finish with lettuce leaves.

Serves 2

Sardine heads were used by the people of ancient Peru to fertilize their nutrient-deficient cornfields.

CURRIED SARDINES ON TOAST

FOR THIS RECIPE, I prefer sardines packed in tomato. Consequently, this concoction goes very well with tomato soup, be it your own homemade version or a quality tinned product. Sardines packed in tomato sauce are considerably lower in fat and richer in omega-3 fatty acids than sardines packed in oil. A much healthier choice!

1	3.75-oz/106 g tin sardines packed in tomato	1
2 tbsp	butter, divided	25 mL
1 1/2 tsp	curry powder plus a couple of pinches for garnish	7 mL
1 tbsp	flour	15 mL
1/4 cup	dry white wine	50 mL
1/2 cup	cream	125 mL
	Salt	
	Fresh ground black pepper	
2	slices multi-grain bread, thinly sliced and toasted	2
1	green onion, the green part thinly sliced	1

In a small saucepan, melt half the butter over medium-high heat. Add the curry powder and the flour. Stir to combine and cook until foamy. Gradually add the wine, stirring constantly. Cook until a smooth paste is formed. Add the cream in a steady stream, stirring constantly to prevent lumps. Continue to cook over medium heat and allow to come to a boil. Reduce heat to minimum while you prepare the remainder of the recipe. Stir occasionally.

Place the oven rack in the highest position and preheat broiler.

Butter the toasted bread with the remaining butter. Top each slice with two sardines, crushing slightly. Remove the backbone if desired. Spoon the prepared curry sauce on top, and garnish each toast slice with green onion and a pinch of curry powder, salt and pepper to taste.

Place under broiler until sauce is bubbly, 2 to 3 minutes, to heat the sardines through.

Serves 1 to 2

SARDINE AND POTATO PANCAKES WITH LEMON AND CHIVE MAYONNAISE

YOU may not think of the humble sardine as exceptionally glamorous, but this recipe will change your way of thinking!

1	3.75-oz/106 g tin sardines, packed in water, drained	1
1	russet potato, grated	1
1	small yellow onion, diced	1
¹/₂ cup	flour	125 mL
1 tsp	baking powder	5 mL
³/₄ cup	buttermilk	175 mL
2 tbsp	vegetable oil	25 mL
1	egg	1
2 tbsp	fresh rosemary, chopped	25 mL
	Fresh ground black pepper	
1 tsp	olive oil	5 mL
1 tsp	butter	5 mL

Mayonnaise:

¹/₂ cup	mayonnaise	125 mL

1 tbsp	lemon juice	15 mL
1 tbsp	chives, chopped	15 mL
	Fresh ground black pepper to taste	

Open tin of sardines, drain and chop into small pieces. Place in medium-size bowl.

Peel the potato, cut it in half and boil for 5 minutes. Remove from water, let dry for 5 to 10 minutes then grate it. Add the potato and onion to chopped sardines.

In another bowl, mix together the flour and baking powder. Whisk in the buttermilk, egg and oil. Combine the two mixtures and season with rosemary and fresh ground pepper.

In a fry pan, melt the butter and oil together over medium heat. When bubbly, pour the potato mixture into the pan, using a soup spoon to make small individual pancakes. When small bubbles form on the top, flip over and cook until golden brown.

To make mayonnaise, mix ingredients in a small bowl. Dollop over the cakes.

Makes 18 small pancakes.

ROAST SARDINES AND LEEKS VINAIGRETTE

ROASTING BRINGS out the unique flavour of the sardines and pairing them with leeks adds an especially sophisticated touch. This vinaigrette goes especially well with mashed potatoes, which absorb all the wonderful juices.

1	3.75-oz/106 g tin sardines packed in mustard	1
2	leeks, sliced	2
1 tbsp	unsalted butter	15 mL
2 tbsp	olive oil	25 mL
1 tbsp	balsamic vinegar	15 mL
	Zest of 1 lemon	
	Salt	
	Fresh ground black pepper	

Preheat oven to 400°F/200°C.

Slice white part of leek into ¼-inch/5 mm slices. Place in a bowl of cold water and toss lightly to loosen any dirt.

Set small fry pan over medium-high heat, add butter and olive oil and heat to melt butter. Lift leeks out of water and shake lightly to remove excess water, add to the pan, stir to coat and cook until leeks begin to fry. Grind the pepper mill three times over the leeks, and place the pan in oven and roast for 10 minutes.

Add whole sardines and toss gently to coat with the leeks, being careful not to break up the sardines. Roast for another 3 minutes to heat sardines through.

Remove from the oven and add the balsamic vinegar and lemon zest. Season with salt and pepper to taste.

Serves 1 to 2 as a small plate

SHRIMP

I TaSTeD SHriMP for the first time at the age of nine. My mother was a lobby hostess at Vancouver's Hotel Georgia and she treated me to shrimp cocktail at the Cavalier Grill. After all these years, it remains one of my most elegant dining experiences. I can still remember the dashing waiters and the white linen tablecloths.

The term *prawn* is often used arbitrarily to describe large shrimp. In fact, the prawn belongs to a specific subgroup of shrimp that are caught in fresh water. Most shrimp are caught in the wild, but within the next decade a third of shrimp processed worldwide are expected to be farm-raised. Wherever it is found, shrimp is every bit as nutritious as any other type of fish but much higher in cholesterol than most – to be avoided by those on cholesterol-reduced diets.

Much as I like tinned shrimp, I cannot tell a lie. Shrimp in the tin is not comparable to fresh shrimp. But when you pair this product with some sumptuous selections from your pantry, a kind of magic happens. You can entertain with the kind of delightful meal that brings to mind a genuine touch of sophistication.

NUGGET POTATOES WITH TARRAGON SHRIMP

THIS DISH IS simple, impressive and especially memorable when the tarragon is fresh from the garden and the nugget potatoes are new.

1	4-oz/113 g tin shrimp	1
½ lb	nugget potatoes	250 g
1 tbsp	butter	15 mL
1 tbsp	olive oil	15 mL
2 tsp	garlic, chopped	10 mL
1 tbsp	fresh tarragon, chopped	15 mL
¼ cup	white wine	50 mL
1	green onion, chopped	1

Steam potatoes for about 10 minutes.

In a medium-size saucepan over medium heat, melt butter and olive oil till bubbling. Add chopped garlic and tarragon. Stir for one minute. Do not allow to brown. Add the shrimp and white wine and heat through.

Slice the potatoes into thirds and cover with sautéed shrimp. Garnish with chopped green onion.

Serves 2 to 3

Who are you calling a shrimp? While some species of shrimp are so tiny that they are barely discernable by the human eye, others can reach quite large proportions, often weighing up to 2 kg (4 lb).

SHRIMP EGG ROLLS

I've created two versions of this recipe, both very tasty. The more exotic variation calls for pear with shisho leaves, which you won't be able to find at every corner store. Most Asian markets stock shisho leaves, however, and the extra effort of hunting them down is worth it.

1	4-oz/113 g tin baby shrimp	1
1 cup	canned crushed pineapple, drained	250 mL
1/4 cup	mayonnaise	50 mL
3 tbsp	cilantro, chopped	45 mL
2 cups	bean sprouts	500 mL
2	green onions, chopped	2
1/2	package 6-inch/15 cm square egg roll wrappers	1/2
1	egg, well beaten	1
	Vegetable oil	

In a small bowl, mix together the shrimp, pineapple, mayonnaise, cilantro, bean sprouts and green onions. Divide mixture into 12 portions.

Lay an egg roll wrapper on a clean work surface so that it looks like a diamond shape. Place one portion of mixture in the centre, fold the point of the wrapper closest to you over the filling. Do the same with the sides. Brush the top point with egg wash, then roll into a tight cylinder. Repeat this process for all 12 portions.

Heat oil in a small pan or wok over medium heat until a strip of egg roll wrapper sizzles when dropped into it and floats to the top immediately. Place 3 or 4 rolls at a time in the hot oil and fry until golden brown on both sides.

Version 2:
Substitute 1 pear, peeled, cut into finger-size pieces and 12 shisho leaves for the pineapple and the cilantro.

Makes 12

SHRIMP AND SWEET POTATO CAKES

AFTER CLOSING my restaurant millions of crab-cakes later, it took awhile before I could make another one. I developed this recipe to prove to myself that I could make a wonderful shrimp cake as well. I'm glad to say that's just what I did.

1	4-oz/113 g tin shrimp	1
¼ cup	sweet potato, grated	50 mL
2	green onions, sliced	2
1	small parsnip, grated	1
1 tbsp	lemon juice	15 mL
¼ tsp	cayenne pepper	1 mL
1	egg, lightly beaten	1
¼ cup	chopped tomato	50 mL
1 tbsp	cilantro, chopped	15 mL
2 tbsp	cornmeal	25 mL
2 tbsp	grated Parmesan cheese	25 mL
1 tbsp	butter	15 mL
1 tbsp	vegetable oil	15 mL

In a bowl, mix together all of the ingredients except the oil and butter. Form into patties and set aside.

Melt butter and oil together in a fry pan over medium heat. When bubbly, place cakes in pan. Turn heat down a little and cook until nicely browned. Turn over with spatula and cook until done, about 2 to 3 minutes.

Serves 2

Unlike its close

relatives, the lobster

and the crab, the shrimp

is primarily a swimmer

rather than a crawler.

SHRIMP AND SPINACH STUFFED TOMATOES

STUFFED TOMATOES may remind you of white gloves and garden parties but this recipe deserves to be appreciated on a more regular basis. If you're in an elegant mood, you can stuff this mixture into cherry tomatoes. If you're having the "good ol' boys" over, use the beefsteak variety. Either way, this recipe makes a nice light luncheon when served with a salad.

1	4-oz/113 g tin shrimp	1
2	cloves garlic, chopped	2
¹/₂	red onion, finely chopped	¹/₂
1 tbsp	olive oil	15 mL
¹/₂ tsp	dried chili flakes	2 mL
1 lb	spinach, steamed and chopped	500 g
¹/₃ cup	ricotta cheese	75 mL
2 tbsp	grated Parmesan cheese	25 mL
	Fresh ground black pepper	
2	tomatoes sliced in half with the flesh and seeds removed	2

Preheat oven to 350°F/180°C. Place rack in the middle of the oven.

In a fry pan over medium heat, sauté the garlic and red onion in the oil with the chili flakes for 1 to 2 minutes. Remove from heat and mix in the shrimp, spinach, ricotta cheese and Parmesan cheese. Season with pepper to taste, then stuff your tomatoes.

Place tomatoes in a casserole dish and bake in the oven for 15 to 20 minutes. Your tomatoes should be nicely browned and bubbly.

Serves 2 to 3

SPANISH RICE
WITH SHRIMP

CALL THIS "LAZY PAELLA." My friends Chico and Leo, who own a charming Spanish tapas bar and are paella aficionados, would frown at this incredibly abbreviated recipe. But there's no denying the flexibility of this savoury treat when you're in a hurry.

1	4-oz/113 g tin shrimp	1
½ cup	prepared spicy salsa	125 mL
¾ cup	arborio rice	175 mL
2 cups	vegetable broth, warmed	500 mL
2	green onions, sliced	2

In a medium-size saucepan over medium heat combine the salsa with the rice. Heat through and add the broth. Bring to a boil and reduce to simmer. Cover and let cook for 20 minutes.

Remove from heat and stir in shrimp and green onions. Serve with salad and bread.

Serves 2

Only about 300 of the several thousand species of shrimp in existence are harvested for human consumption.

ASIAN SHRIMP STIR FRY

THere are few things in a kitchen that are more fun to cook with than a wok. In less time than it takes to think about ordering take-out Chinese food, you could have finished this dish and felt so much the better for it.

1	4-oz/113 g tin shrimp	1
1 tbsp	sesame oil	15 mL
½ lb	oyster mushrooms	250 g
1	bok choy, sliced thin	1
3	green onions, sliced	3
¼ lb	snow peas	125 g
1 tbsp	light soy sauce	15 mL

In a wok, heat the oil over medium to high heat.
Add the mushrooms and bok choy and sauté for 1
minute. Add the green onions, snow peas, shrimp
and soy sauce and sauté together for 1 to 2 minutes.

Serve over cooked rice or rice noodles. You
may spice this dish up with chili peppers if
desired.

Serves 2

The very first cans

were oval in shape.

These, however, proved

to be unsuccessful and

were soon replaced by

the cylinder-shaped

cans that we are

familiar with today.

PASTA RAMEKINS WITH SHRIMP AND GOAT CHEESE

I have made this dish without shrimp with great success for many years. Recently, I threw in some tinned shrimp on a whim guessing that it would make the recipe even better. According to my party guests, my instincts were right. You can find fresh pasta sheets in the fresh pasta section of most supermarkets.

1	4-oz/113 g tin shrimp	1
2	fresh pasta sheets	2
3 to 4 tbsp	melted butter	45 to 50 mL
3 to 4 tbsp	grated Parmesan cheese	45 to 50 mL
5 oz	goat cheese	142 g
1	egg	1
2 tbsp	heavy cream	25 mL
3	sun-dried tomatoes, thinly sliced	3
3	fresh basil leaves, chopped	3

Preheat oven to 350°F/180°C.

Using a ramekin dish, trace onto your pasta sheet 4 circles with the open end of the dish and 4 circles with the closed end.

Coat 4 ramekin dishes with some of the melted butter and Parmesan cheese. Place one large pasta circle in each dish. Fit snugly.

In a bowl, mix the goat cheese, egg and cream until well combined. Add the tomatoes, basil and shrimp and mix well.

Place mixture into lined ramekins. Top each with smaller pasta circle, brush with melted butter and sprinkle remaining Parmesan cheese on top.

Bake for 15 to 20 minutes. Remove from oven, run knife gently around edge of dish and overturn onto desired serving dish.

Try serving this on a bed of wild greens that has been tossed with a bal-samic vinaigrette.

Serves 4

SHRIMP AND DILL QUICHE

THE COMBINATION of shrimp and dill is truly a classic taste. What makes this recipe a little different is the addition of feta cheese. For an additional dash of Greek flair, try adding sliced black olives.

1	4-oz/113 g tin shrimp	1
1	9-inch/23 cm pastry shell	1
1 cup	crumbled feta cheese	250 mL
1/4 cup	chopped green onions	50 mL
2 tbsp	fresh dill, chopped or 2 tsp/10 mL dried	25 mL
2	large eggs	2
1 cup	light cream	250 mL
	Fresh ground black pepper	
1/4 cup	grated Parmesan cheese	50 mL

Preheat oven to 375°F/190°C.

Bake pastry shell for 10 minutes. Remove shell from oven and lower heat to 350°F/180°C.

Distribute shrimp on pastry, followed by the feta cheese, green onions and dill.

In a bowl, whisk together the eggs, cream and black pepper to taste. Pour over the mixture and sprinkle with Parmesan cheese. Bake for 40 minutes. Let sit for a few minutes before serving.

Serves 2 to 3

Five billion pounds of shrimp are produced worldwide each year. The top five shrimp-producing countries in the world are China, Indonesia, Thailand, Ecuador and India.

TOASTED SHRIMP SANDWICH WITH CARROTS AND HAZELNUTS

I've adapted this recipe from an old cookbook put together by my mother's church women's auxiliary group back in the fifties. It's a nice change from a tuna sandwich while providing the same sense of comfort.

1	4-oz/113 g tin shrimp	1
1	medium carrot, grated	1
1/4 cup	hazelnuts, chopped	50 mL
2 tbsp	mayonnaise	25 mL
1 tsp	lemon juice	5 mL
	Dash cayenne pepper	
4	slices multi-grain bread, toasted	4
1 cup	iceberg lettuce, shredded	250 mL

In bowl, mix together the shrimp, carrot and hazelnuts. Add the mayonnaise, lemon juice and cayenne pepper and blend well, but gently.

Lay out your toast. Divide the lettuce between 2 slices, top with the shrimp mixture, cover with the other slice, cut into 2 and serve.

Serves 2

TUNA

GROWING UP, most of us recall tuna as the main ingredient in two classic recipes: the tuna sandwich and the tuna casserole. To this day, the only drawback with the tuna casserole is that you can't wrap it with paper and take it to school. That's where the tuna sandwich comes in. As a child, it was my favourite brown bag lunch and I practised mixing together the right combination of tuna, celery and green onion until I achieved the perfect balance. Other kids would attempt to trade their chicken sandwiches for it, sometimes offering to throw in a cookie or an apple. Of course, I always refused.

Remember those ads that referred to tinned tuna as Chicken of the Sea? Well, I always thought that was an insult to the unique flavour of tuna. After all, tuna has a noble history. Preserving the fish, drying it in small cubes or pickling it in brine goes back to 525 BC, and early recipes used seasonings such as cinnamon, coriander, vinegar and honey. Canning tuna started in the late 1800s, providing a taste and convenience that has satisfied millions around the world. If you're still wondering why anyone would go to all the trouble to preserve tuna, then you've never been to my place for a tuna melt.

You may have gathered by now that I'm a bit of a tuna snob. I stick to the albacore (white meat) species for all my recipes. I don't mean to put down all the other varieties of tinned tuna, but I find the chunk form brings out all the best qualities that the fish has to offer. When purchasing tinned tuna, you should also consider what it's packed in. I buy tuna packed in water since this maintains the true flavour of the fish better than oil or brine. Besides, the oil tends to draw away up to a third of the nutrients from the fish, as well as boosting the number of fat-based calories.

The great thing about tuna is that its true flavour will always come through in any number of recipes. What does tuna marry well with? Just about everything. In the following selection of recipes, I include tuna with pasta, potatoes, rice and all varieties of vegetables, herbs and spices. And so, with this selection, I happily liberate tuna in the tin from the comforting confines of the brown bag and the casserole dish. Enjoy.

TUNA FISH AND
POTATO CASSEROLE

MY mother made this recipe with yellow onions sliced in rings and Campbell's Mushroom Soup. When I tried it for myself, I had to do it my own way. The use of heavy cream in this recipe is not mandatory, but it does quicken the procedure. Regular or skim milk can be used, if you want less fat. I even tried it once with soy milk.

1	6-oz/170 g tin tuna, drained and flaked	1
8	small potatoes, sliced 1/8-inch/2 mm thick	8
8	garlic cloves, peeled	8
10	pearl onions, peeled	10
	Fresh ground black pepper	
1 tbsp	olive oil	15 mL
1 1/2 tsp	lemon juice	7 mL
1/2 tsp	chopped fresh rosemary or 1/4 tsp/1 mL dried rosemary	2 mL
1/2 tsp	chopped fresh thyme or 1/4 tsp/1 mL dried thyme	2 mL
1/2 tbsp	butter	7 mL
1/2 lb	mushrooms, sliced	250 g
2 tbsp	vegetable stock	25 mL
1 cup	heavy cream	250 mL
1/2 cup	grated Parmesan cheese	125 mL

Preheat oven to 350°F/180°C. Place rack in the middle of the oven.

Using an 11-inch/ 3 L casserole dish, place sliced potatoes, peeled garlic and pearl onions in dish. Toss with ground pepper (to taste), olive oil, lemon juice, rosemary and thyme. Cover with lid or aluminum foil and bake for 20 minutes.

Over medium to high heat, melt butter in a medium-size saucepan. Lower heat to medium, add sliced mushrooms and sauté for 5 minutes. Add vegetable stock and half the cream, let reduce for 2 to 3 minutes and then add the other half. Reduce sauce to a nice consistency, not too thick, not too thin.

Remove potatoes from oven. Place flaked tuna in pieces on top of potato mixture. Cover with mushroom sauce, then sprinkle Parmesan cheese on top. Place cover on casserole, and bake in oven for 15 minutes.

Test potatoes with fork. When cooked, remove cover for 3 to 5 minutes and let casserole bubble and brown.

Serves 2 to 3

TUNA AND ARTICHOKE SALAD

In 1983, I visited New York City for the specific purpose of discovering unique food products. I spotted my first bottle of balsamic vinegar, which I smuggled home in my suitcase. Of course now, most pantries include this delightful product. The use of balsamic vinegar in this recipe adds an Italian flourish. And to think I used to believe that the only reason to visit Modena (the birthplace of balsamic vinegar) was to stalk Pavarotti!

1	6-oz/170 g tin tuna, drained	1
2 tsp	balsamic vinegar	10 mL
2 tbsp	mayonnaise	25 mL
1 tsp	lemon juice	5 mL
1	14-oz/398 mL tin artichokes, drained and each heart cut into 4 pieces	1
2	green onions, sliced	2
2 tbsp	pitted black olives, sliced	25 mL
3	fresh basil leaves	3
3	sun-dried tomatoes, sliced	3
	Fresh ground black pepper	

In a medium-size bowl, mix together the balsamic vinegar, mayonnaise and lemon juice.

Place all other ingredients in the dressing and toss gently. Add fresh ground pepper to taste.

Arrange mixture on a bed of butter lettuce or chopped romaine lettuce and serve. To make a nice lunch, serve with a hearty multi-grain bread.

Serves 2 to 3

Tuna – the largest member of the mackerel family – was caught and consumed by the Phoenicians 3,000 years ago. Believing that its tail brought good luck, they hung up this posterior part of the fish and devoured the rest.

NEW YORK LUNCH

IN MY MIND, New York City and tuna are the perfect match. I have fond memories of visiting Manhattan's Frick Museum, heading off to a deli for a tuna fix and eating lunch on the steps of a brownstone. I remember feeling so very alive and happy at that moment. Was it the tuna or was it New York? This simple recipe, written down exactly as I remember it, proves that it very well could have been the tuna.

1	6-oz/170 g tin tuna, drained	1
3/4 cup	small pasta shells	175 mL
1/2 cup	fresh peas, lightly steamed	125 mL
2 to 3	green onions, sliced	2 to 3
1/3 cup	diced red pepper	75 mL

Dressing:

1 tbsp	white wine vinegar	15 mL
3 tbsp	olive oil	45 mL
	Pinch salt	
	Fresh ground black pepper	
	Pinch each of tarragon, marjoram and thyme (fresh or dried)	
1 tbsp	chopped fresh parsley	15 mL

To prepare dressing, place all ingredients in a small jar and shake well.

Cook the pasta shells according to package directions. Drain and rinse with cold water.

Place the pasta, tuna, peas, red pepper and green onions together in bowl. Toss with dressing.

This recipe tastes best after 1 to 2 hours in the refrigerator.

Serves 2

Tuna packed in brine was once a crucial part of Mediterranean trade. So much so that the fish was featured on the coins of ancient Carthage and of Cadiz in Spain.

APPLE, CHEDDAR AND TUNA MELT

IN HIGH SCHOOL, one of the first things I learned to make was the classic Tuna Melt. Proudly heading home to show off my culinary achievement to mother, I made several Tuna Melts and promptly devoured most of them. It took awhile before I could look at a Tuna Melt again, but this version rekindled my love affair.

1	6-oz/170 g tin tuna, drained	1
1 tbsp	mayonnaise	15 mL
1 tsp	lemon juice	5 mL
1/4 cup	celery, diced	50 mL
1/4 cup	diced red onion	50 mL
1	Granny Smith apple, peeled and chopped into small cubes	1
	Fresh ground black pepper	
	Sourdough baguette	
3/4 cup	grated Cheddar cheese	175 mL

Place tuna in a medium-size bowl. Add mayonnaise (you may want a little more than my desired amount), lemon juice, red onion, celery and apple. Grind the pepper in to taste. Combine well.

Slice 8 slices from the baguette, about ¹/₂-inch/ 1 cm thick. Cover baguette slices with the mixture, then sprinkle each slice with the Cheddar cheese.

Place rack in top portion of oven and turn on broiler. Place the slices on a cookie sheet and put under broiler for 2 to 3 minutes. You want your cheese to be bubbly and brown, but not burnt, and you want the slices to be warmed through.

Serves 2 to 3

In North America only five of the 13 species of tuna are harvested commercially: albacore, yellowfin, bluefin, bigeye and skipjack. Of these, only those tins with albacore are labelled "white meat tuna."

YAM, RED PEPPER AND TUNA CASSEROLE

THIS casserole follows the same procedures as the Tuna Fish and Potato Casserole (p. 142), but with different ingredients. Just another twist. Yams make this recipe special. Although their taste makes them seem deceptively high in calories, they are a good source of beta-carotene and vitamins A and B.

1	6-oz/170 g tin tuna, drained	1
1	large yam, sliced into 1/4-inch/5 mm rounds	1
1/2	medium red onion, sliced into rings	1/2
1/2	medium red pepper, cut into chunks	1/2
1 tbsp	chopped fresh basil or 1 tsp/5 mL dried	15 mL
	Fresh ground black pepper	
1 1/2 tsp	olive oil	7 mL
1 1/2 tsp	balsamic vinegar	7 mL
1 1/2 tsp	lemon juice	7 mL
1 tbsp	butter	15 mL
1 tbsp	flour	15 mL
1 cup	milk	250 mL
1/2 cup	grated Parmesan cheese	125 mL

Aloha tuna!

In Hawaii, where a

great deal of tuna is

caught, albacore is

known as *tombo,*

yellowfin as *ahi* **and**

skipjack as *aku.*

Preheat oven to 350°F/180°C.

Place yam, red onion, red pepper, basil and
fresh ground pepper in an 11-inch/3 L casserole
dish. Blend oil, balsamic vinegar and lemon juice and combine gently with
the vegetables. Cover with lid or aluminum foil and bake in the oven for 15
to 20 minutes.

In saucepan over medium heat, melt butter. Add flour and stir well with
wooden spoon for 30 seconds; do not brown. Add milk slowly, stirring constantly. When mixture has reached a medium-thick consistency, add cheese.
Stir until well blended, about 30 seconds. Remove from heat.

Remove vegetables from oven and place drained tuna in pieces on top.
Pour cheese sauce over all. (If sauce has become too thick, add a little warm
milk to thin.) Grind pepper on top to taste.

Bake covered for 10 to 15 minutes, then uncovered for 5 minutes to
bubble and brown.

Serves 2 to 3

TUNA AND CANNELI
BEANS IN PITA POCKETS

In the last decade or so, the pita pocket has become a popular substitute for sliced bread. Snipping off the top and stuffing the pocket with an appetizing combination of ingredients is the ultimate in dining convenience. While the filling for this recipe is messy, the pita pocket provides the perfect solution.

1	6-oz/170 g tin tuna, drained	1
½ cup	cooked or canned canneli beans (drained if canned)	125 mL
¼	celery, diced	50 mL
¼	green onions, chopped	50 mL
¼	red pepper, diced	50 mL
6	mini pitas (about 4-inch/10 cm rounds)	6

Dressing:

½ tsp	cumin	2 mL
1 tbsp	lemon juice	15 mL
2 tbsp	olive oil	25 mL
	Fresh ground black pepper	

To prepare dressing, place cumin, lemon juice, olive oil and pepper in a jar or bowl. Whisk or shake together. Set aside.

In a bowl, combine the tuna, beans, celery, green onions and red pepper. Add the dressing and mix together. Snip off the top of the pitas and fill. Serve at once.

Serves 2 to 3

Apparently the oval cans that were filled with fish for the Gold Rush miners of 1849 are the very "herring boxes without topses" worn as slippers by "My Darling Clementine."

AVOCADO, TUNA AND CORN RELISH PITA

THIS IS Tuna with a southwestern flair. Pairing tuna with avocado was such an easy thing to do. And as with the Tuna and Canneli Beans (p. 152), the best way to eat this mixture is in a pita pocket.

1	6-oz/170 g tin tuna, drained	1
1	ripe avocado, peeled and cut into cubes	1
1/3 cup	kernel corn	75 mL
1/4 cup	tomato, diced	50 mL
1/4 cup	red onion, finely chopped	50 mL
1/2 tsp	jalapeño pepper, chopped (no seeds)	2 mL
1/4 cup	red pepper, diced (no seeds)	50 mL
1 tbsp	lime juice	15 mL
1 tbsp	olive oil	15 mL
1 1/2 tsp	cilantro, minced	7 mL
	Pinch salt	
	Fresh ground black pepper to taste	
6	mini pitas (about 4-inch/10 cm rounds)	6

Put all ingredients except mini pitas in a bowl and mix gently until well combined. You may want to add a little more lime juice and olive oil.

Fill your pitas and serve.

Serves 2 to 3

Of the 600,000 tons of

tuna consumed in North

America each year, less

than 5% is fresh tuna.

SESAME, GREEN BEANS AND TUNA SALAD

THIS salad IS designed as a light summer
meal with a loaf of good bread. But it also is a welcome addition to any buffet featuring an array of
interesting salads.

1	6-oz/170 g tin tun, drained	1
1 lb	green beans, trimmed and sliced on the diagonal into 3 pieces	500 g
1	small red pepper, sliced into strips	1
1 tbsp	sesame seeds (roasted if desired)	15 mL
	Sliced green onions	

Dressing:

2 tbsp	Japanese soy sauce	25 mL
1 tbsp	sesame oil	15 mL
2 tbsp	sherry	25 mL
3 tbsp	olive oil	45 mL
1 tsp	brown sugar	5 mL
1/2 tsp	minced ginger	2 mL
	Salt	
	Fresh ground black pepper	

To prepare dressing, place all ingredients in a jar and shake well.

Steam the beans for just over 1 minute and then toss with the dressing and the red pepper.

Chill in the refrigerator for an hour or more. Just before serving, toss with the tuna chunks and sprinkle the sesame seeds over all. Place the green onions on top.

Serves 3 to 4

Sorry Charlie! For years StarKist's principal advertising icon was Charlie, an erudite tuna. In his ceaseless efforts to be harvested by StarKist, Charlie tried to impress the company with his taste in poetry and classical music, but he always received the same response: "Sorry, Charlie. StarKist doesn't want tuna with good taste, StarKist wants tuna that tastes good."

TUNA AND
RICE CASSEROLE

Tuna casserole to most people means one
of three things: with potatoes, with pasta or with rice.
My mother made it with potatoes. I find this rice version much more appealing.

2	6-oz/170 g tins tuna	2
4 tbsp	butter, divided	50 mL
1 cup	basmati rice	250 mL
1/3 cup	golden raisins	75 mL
2 1/2 cups	vegetable stock	625 mL
2 tsp	curry powder	10 mL
1/4 tsp	ground ginger	1 mL
1 cup	mushrooms, sliced	250 mL
1/4 cup	dry white wine	50 mL
1/4 tsp	dry mustard	1 mL
1 1/3 cup	heavy cream	325 mL
2	green onions, sliced	2
3/4 cup	grated Parmesan cheese	175 mL
	Fresh ground black pepper	

Preheat oven to 375°F/190°C.

In a medium-size saucepan, heat 2 tbsp of the butter. Add rice and stir until well coated. Add raisins and vegetable stock. Bring to a boil. Turn down heat, cover and simmer for 20 minutes.

Butter a 13-inch/3.5 L casserole dish. When rice is cooked, spread over the bottom of the dish. Place tuna over the rice mixture.

In a skillet over medium to low heat, melt the remaining 2 tbsp butter. Add curry powder and ginger, stir for 20 seconds then add the mushrooms. Simmer gently for 3 minutes and then add the white wine. Sprinkle in the dry mustard, stir until well combined and the wine has slightly reduced. Slowly add the heavy cream while stirring constantly until mixture reaches a medium to thick consistency.

Remove from heat, add sliced green onions and spoon over the tuna and rice. Top with grated Parmesan cheese, ground black pepper and bake in oven for 20 minutes.

Serves 4

TUNA AND PASTA CASEROLE

MY nephew, Dylan, does not like potatoes or rice, so I created this dish for him. It could have a number of different ingredients added to it, but this is how Dylan likes it! This recipe is particularly rich in calcium — great for combatting osteoporosis — because of the inclusion of both milk and cheese.

1	6-oz/170 g tin tuna, drained and flaked	1
1 tbsp	butter	15 mL
1 tbsp	flour	15 mL
1 cup	milk	250 mL
1 cup	grated Cheddar cheese	250 mL
1/2	package broad egg noodles	1/2
1/3 cup	grated Parmesan cheese	75 mL
	Fresh ground black pepper	

In a medium-size saucepan over medium heat, melt butter. Add flour and stir for about 1 minute. Slowly add milk until sauce reaches a nice medium-thick consistency. Remove from heat, add grated Cheddar cheese and stir until well combined.

Meanwhile in another saucepan, cook the noodles according to package directions.

Butter an 11-inch/3 L casserole dish and lay the cooked noodles in the dish. Cover the noodles with the tuna. Cover with the cheese sauce. Sprinkle the Parmesan cheese over all. Grind black pepper on top and bake for 10 minutes until warmed through and bubbly and brown on the top.

Serves 3 to 4

Today most people make sure that their tin of tuna has a dolphin-safe symbol somewhere on the label. In 1990 North American tuna canners responded to one of history's most widespread consumer boycotts by announcing that they would no longer buy tuna that had been caught using drift nets, a fishing method that led to the drowning of millions of dolphins.

THE PANTRY

When I came up with the idea for this book, my plan was to make both the recipes and their ingredients as accessible as possible. For example, I have not included recipes for pastry, mayonnaise or special sauces, because they are more time-consuming and difficult to whip up at the last moment. With this approach in mind, here is a list of handy items that, with the addition of tin fish, make up a well-stocked cupboard.

In the Cupboard

Artichoke Hearts (in water)
Kidney Beans
Tomato Paste
Roma Tomatoes
Pimentos
Sun-Dried Tomatoes
Pitted Black Olives
Pesto Sauce
Rice
Chick Peas
Olive Oil
Vegetable Oil
Balsamic Vinegar
Flour
Sherry (dry)
Worcestershire Sauce
Bread Crumbs
Pine Nuts
Sesame Oil
Soy Sauce
Cornmeal
Baking Powder
Salsa

In the Refrigerator

Fresh Tomatoes (they really shouldn't go in the refrigerator, but you know what I mean)
Horseradish
Green Onions
Parmesan Cheese
Cheddar Cheese
Goat Cheese
Cream Cheese
Eggs
Garlic
Parsley
Potatoes
Carrots
Yellow and Red Onions
Mayonnaise
Butter
Celery
Lemons
Dry White Wine
Chives
Spinach

On the Spice Shelf

Rosemary
Basil
Sea Salt
Pepper
Cayenne Pepper
Curry Powder
Cumin
Dried Chilies
Tarragon
Dill

In the Freezer

Phyllo Pastry
Puff Pastry
Pizza Dough
Frozen Peas
Frozen Corn
Stock (frozen in small batches)
Egg Roll Wrappers

INDEX TO RECIPES

DIANE CLEMENT
AT THE TOMATO

Recipes and Tales from the
Tomato Fresh Food Café

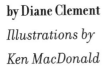 **with a new introduction
and all the old magic**

by Diane Clement

Illustrations by
Ken MacDonald

176 pages
more than 35 b&w illustrations,
softbound, lay-flat binding
ISBN 1-895714-95-8
$15.95 CDN, $12.95 US

RAINCOAST BOOKS

8680 Cambie Street
Vancouver, B.C. V6P 6M9
1-800-663-5714

To order in the U.S., call
Orca Book Publishers at
1-800-210-5277

VANCOUVER'S
TOMATO FRESH
FOOD CAFÉ
is one of the city's coolest eateries and
meeting places for writers, actors, artists,
athletes, musicians and all those who love
home-cooking sprinkled with West Coast
panache. In *At the Tomato* Diane Clement,
former Olympic sprinter and bestselling
cookbook author, reveals the secrets of the
café's success with a unique combination
of recipes, whimsical anecdotes, choice
behind-the-scenes tales and engaging line
drawings by stage designer and artist Ken
MacDonald. Good, healthy eating is definitely the main attraction in this unusually
entertaining cookbook, and those who love
great food will find this collection of basic
recipes spiced with international flavours
a treat for reading and cooking.